Library of
Davidson College

.31 → Men against rev.

Lenin and the Myth of World Revolution:

Ideology and Reasons of State, 1917–1920

Piero Melograni

Translated by

Julie Lerro

HUMANITIES PRESS INTERNATIONAL, INC.
Atlantic Highlands, NJ

Originally published as *Il Mito Della Rivoluzione Mondiale: Lenin Tra Ideologia e Ragion di Stato, 1917–1920,* © 1985 Gius. Laterza & Figli Spa, Roma-Bari

First Published in 1989 by
Humanities Press International, Inc.,
Atlantic Highlands, NJ 07716

©Piero Melograni, 1989

Library of Congress Cataloging-in-Publication Data
Melograni, Piero.
   Lenin and the myth of world revolution.
   Includes bibliographies and index.
   Translation of: Il mito della rivoluzione mondiale.
   1. Revolutions and socialism. 2. Lenin, Vladimir Il'ich, 1870–1924.
3. Soviet Union — Foreign relations —
1917–1945. I. Title.
HX550.R48M4513   1989   320.5'322   88-13334
ISBN 0-391-03610-6

All rights reserved. No reproduction, copy or transmission of this publication may be made without written permission.

Printed in the United States of America

to Giulietta

Contents

Author's Preface to the English Edition ... ix

Preface to the First Edition ... xi

1. The Brest-Litovsk Accord ... 1
2. Lenin Aided by the Kaiser ... 9
3. The German Bourgeoisie's Preference for the Bolsheviks ... 15
4. The Berlin Treaties ... 21
5. The Hostility between Lenin and Rosa Luxemburg ... 27
6. Russia's Difference ... 37
7. Lenin Seeks an Accord with the Victors ... 43
8. Bullitt's Mission ... 49
9. The Founding of the Comintern ... 55
10. The Revolution in Hungary ... 59
11. Germany and Russia Resume Relations ... 63
12. Radek's "Political Salon" ... 67
13. Lenin and the Italian Revolutionaries ... 71
14. Bolshevism and Asia ... 77
15. London Fears the Russian Threat ... 83
16. End of the Economic Blockade ... 91
17. The War between Russia and Poland ... 97
18. Lloyd George Receives Krasin at 10 Downing Street ... 103
19. Warsaw in Danger ... 111
20. Russia in the International Community ... 119

List of Abbreviations ... 125

Notes	125
Select Bibliography	151
Index	157

Author's Preface to the English Edition

The text of the English version of my book is exactly the same as the original Italian edition published in 1985. I have felt no need to change anything. What I have read on the same subject over the past four years has only served to confirm the convictions I expressed then.

The book's main theory is that Lenin did not want world revolution. I do not mean to imply that he was a moderate, however. Quite the contrary. I would simply like to offer a new viewpoint from which to reflect on the policies Lenin resorted to in his desire to strengthen the Soviet State. This may also provide a better understanding of the elements of continuity that exist between Lenin's policies and those of his successors.

When this book was first published four years ago, it evoked lively criticism in the Italian press. Most reviewers, however, did not object to the book's main theory. The communists, who did not agree, chose to remain silent. With the publication of the English edition, I am submitting my convictions to the judgment of a much wider audience, and I do hope to find this audience more disposed to challenge my ideas. After all, if the book's hypotheses are well-founded, a part of twentieth–century history ought to be interpreted differently; and a new interpretation will take hold only if it is able to stand up under heavy scrutiny.

I would like to give my special thanks to Julie Lerro for her patience in translating my Italian, and to Cristina Scatamacchia and Barbara Curli for help in editing notes.

Preface to the First Edition

In 1917 Lenin wrote a well-known book entitled *The State and Revolution*. At the end of that same year, he came to power and set up a state that was totally different from the utopian model described in his book. In fact, from the beginning the state established by the chief of the Bolsheviks was a "state without revolution." Not only did it block the revolutionary aspirations of Russian socialism, but it was also a state that looked inward, that closed itself up in its diversity, that gave up its designs of global revolution. The Russian revolution did not act as a spark that set off European revolutionary uprisings. Although it is often said that Lenin's state lasted "in spite of the fact" that no European revolution broke out, it could be argued that the Bolsheviks' power survived "exactly because" there were no revolutions in the countries that were more industrialized than Russia.

Over the years, communists in the industrial countries of the West have often manifested a guilt complex over the fact that they were unable to help the Bolsheviks by fomenting revolutions in their own countries. This book may free them from this complex. But it will raise other disquieting questions in their minds about the myth of Lenin as well as the nature of communism and its *raison d'être*.

Lenin conceived the idea of "socialism in only one country" from the moment he took power. But he could not make it explicit because it would not have been readily accepted by his comrades. The head of Bolshevism had to wait for the opportune moment. That moment was to come, however, only after his own death in December 1924, when Stalin publicly affirmed that "the victory of socialism in one sole country, even though that country is less capitalistically developed and even though capitalism continues to survive in other countries, is perfectly possible and probable."

Though Lenin realized that a socialist revolution in the more economically developed countries was highly unlikely, he might not even have wanted one. He knew that a revolutionary uprising in Germany or some other European country could create serious problems for Russian Bolshevism. The socialist parties in Germany and other industrial countries were very different from the Bolshevik party; they were more modern and democratic. If they had come to power, they would have founded their power on countries that were stronger and more advanced than Russia, and their strength would have irreparably weakened Bolshevik hegemony over the European Left. The sharp dissension between Lenin and Rosa Luxemburg showed how great the contrasts over this hegemony could be between Russian Bolsheviks and the socialists from the more industrialized countries.

Furthermore, a revolution in a major European country might have induced the great powers to form an alliance against the Soviets and go to war. Communist historians have always claimed that from the beginning the capitalist countries were at war with Soviet Russia, but the facts prove the contrary. Although the great Western powers sent aid to the White Russian Army and military divisions to various parts of the ex-czarist empire, Germany did sign an agreement with Lenin in 1918. Moreover, the countries of the Entente had always been afraid of getting involved in a war on Russia's vast territory. A revolution in a major European country might have helped the Entente nations overcome their fears about such a war.

Those who state that Lenin continued to believe that world revolution was imminent from 1917 to 1920 are implying that he was an inept politician who committed a fundamental error in foreseeing future events, thus misleading himself and others over a long period of time. This book expounds the theory that Lenin, on the contrary, had no illusions. He was a realist; that was how he held on to power.

It is true that Lenin's ideas differed from those of many other Bolshevik leaders and from the mass of followers, who continued hoping for world revolution. But the main purpose here is establishing what Lenin himself thought rather than what his aides and followers thought or hoped. Within the Soviet state and outside of it, there was a great difference between what was happening in diplomatic circles and what public opinion, or a good part of it, believed was going on. On the diplomatic level, leaders and statesmen quickly realized that Lenin foresaw many years of coexistence. Those who were less cunning did not understand the situation and ingenuously believed in "appearances." It would be inexcusable, however, if historians continued to believe in them after so many years.

If I succeed in proving my hypothesis, a few significant events of recent times will have to be seen in new light. To begin with, the statement made in many history texts that Lenin immediately wanted to set the world on fire will need to be corrected. The Third International will also have to be reinterpreted. In fact, it was not founded to export revolution, but simply to defend one state.

One could observe that Lenin thought the Bolsheviks might incite global revolution a few decades later, after they had consolidated their position at home. This theory, however, does not contradict my assumption. First, because it means that he considered revolution in Europe subordinate to the interests of Soviet Russia. Second, because Lenin, who was 47 years old in

1917, could not have realistically forecast what would occur decades after his death. I am not trying to affirm that once Lenin took power he necessarily renounced the idea of the future success of communism around the globe. Not at all. What I mean to affirm is that he put it off indefinitely, and decided to prepare the way for this success by following a road that was decidedly different from that of European socialism. Probably Lenin himself realized the risks of his choice to go "the Russian way," but it is also likely that he believed he had no other choice. Even before 1917 Russian Leninism showed signs of being profoundly different from European socialism.

In 1917–20, however, almost all the Russian revolutionaries, including some Bolsheviks, believed that without the immediate support of a revolution in the industrial countries, the new Bolshevik state would become an anomaly, a sort of prison, or a total failure of democratic socialism. That is exactly what happened. The international communist movement was founded to protect this failure; and it still does so today, going as far as to proclaim that the hopes of the world are to be found in it. The Italian Communist party seems less and less convinced of this argument; and yet not even this party has dared to look too closely at the history of the Third International or to criticize Leninism and recognize its failure. The international communist movement claimed that it was destined to become the symbol of the future. The facts show that the theories and practice of Leninism have made communist takeovers possible only in places that were prevalently rural societies in decline: Russia, China, Yugoslavia, Cuba, and Vietnam.

In expounding my theory, I have not written a complete history of Lenin's foreign policy, as that was not my aim. I only want to demonstrate the specific point of Lenin's renunciation of world revolution, and I have limited myself to documentation sufficient for that purpose. Thus, I have omitted many documents and have left out the description of events that would only repeat points already made and make for heavy reading.

I have already published two studies on Lenin and revolution in the West. The first, "Lenin e la Prospettiva Rivoluzionaria in Italia" ("Lenin and Prospects for Revolution in Italy"), which came out in 1978, has been reprinted twice, and has given rise to lively criticism.* The second essay, "Lenin e la Rivoluzione Mondiale" ("Lenin and World Revolution"),

---

*My essay "Lenin e la Prospettiva Rivoluzionaria in Italia" was published in *Rivoluzione e Reazione in Europa, 1917–1924*, vol. 2 (Rome, 1978), pp. 281ff. The essay appeared also in *Mondoperaio* (May 1978): 89–98. Finally, it was reprinted in my collection of essays *Fascismo, Comunismo e Rivoluzione Industriale* (Rome-Bari, 1984), pp. 84ff. For the criticism it evoked, see my comment in *Storia Contemporanea*, 11, no. 1 (1980): 127ff. The second essay, "Lenin e la Rivoluzione Mondiale," appeared in *Mondoperaio*, (July–August 1981): 111ff.

appeared in 1981 and was a preliminary discussion of the thesis set forth in this book. In the 1978 essay, I already felt I could affirm that Lenin did not worry about delaying revolution in the West because he had already given up on that revolution. His objective was to create communist parties in the West that were totally loyal, disciplined, and subordinate to the needs of the Soviet state.

This book has been a number of years in the making, and I have been thinking about the subject for a long time. In the course of my research, I was awarded a study grant in 1980 by the Woodrow Wilson International Center for Scholars in Washington, D.C., headed by James H. Billington. This book would never have seen the light if it were not for the unique opportunity that the center offered me. I am also grateful to the Fulbright Commission, directed by Cipriana Scelba in Italy, that granted me a post-graduate scholarship on the same occasion.

1

The Brest-Litovsk Accord

When Lenin came to power, during the First World War, the czarist empire was still primarily a rural society. About 75 percent of the working population was peasant-farmers, 16 percent was employed in service jobs, and only 9 percent worked in industry and construction. Industrial "take-off" had already begun, but industrialization was still in its infancy. The Russian working class was still quite small, and an orthodox Marxist would not have considered the country ready for proletarian revolution. Lenin, who was not an orthodox Marxist, was of another mind. *"On s'engage et puis . . . on voit"* ("You start and then you wait and see"), Napoleon had said, and in 1917 Lenin repeated it.[1]

In the Italian newspaper *Avanti!*, on 24 December 1917, Antonio Gramsci greeted the Bolshevik revolution as "a revolution against Capital" — not capital with a small letter *c* (the capital of the bourgeoisie), but *Capital* — that is, Karl Marx's *Capital*. "The Bolsheviks disavow Karl Marx," Gramsci frankly declared. The facts of revolution went beyond the ideologies. But Gramsci wanted to believe that the Bolsheviks would succeed in recomposing the facts and the ideologies into a new, harmonious form.

The truth is that the Bolshevik party was small, not homogeneous, and basically unprepared to run a government. In January 1917, out of a population of 140 million inhabitants, there were little more than 20,000 registered party members. In the course of a year they were to become more than 100,000, but that was still not enough to give rise to a new ruling class. Many of the newer members had joined the party under the euphoric influence of the revolution; they did not have a real feeling for politics. Even most of the old-time Bolsheviks were unsuited to the function of governing. Their experience as clandestine conspirators and émigrés had made them better at destroying than building. "We are not often short of propagandists," Lenin declared on 27 November 1918, "but our most crying shortage is the lack of efficient leaders and organizers."[2]

In November 1917,* Russia was overwhelmed by political, economic, and military upheavals of enormous proportions. It was also at war with Germany, Austria-Hungary, and Turkey. The Bolsheviks were well aware of how precarious their hold on power was, and in order to strengthen it many of them were counting on world revolution. Almost all the Bolsheviks thought that Soviet Russia would survive only if revolution rapidly spread to Europe's industrial countries. Their hopes for a quickly spreading revolutionary flame seemed justified because, in that dramatic year, all of Europe was shaken not only by a large-scale war but also by alarming social unrest.

When Lenin came to power, he did not share all the hopes of his comrades, just as he did not share their opinion about a close connection between the Bolshevik revolution and world revolution. At a meeting of the Bolshevik Central Committee held on 29 October 1917, Lenin did not paint a very optimistic picture of the situation in Europe. He stated that in Germany "things were rather far along" and that the European proletariat was "on the side" of the Bolshevik revolution; but his analysis of the European situation led him to "demonstrate that revolution was more difficult there than in Russia."[3]

The circumstances that had convinced Lenin to seize power had little to do with global revolution. In the first place, he felt that even if power could not be held for long, the experience should still be tried. The 1871 Commune of Paris had lasted only a few weeks, but in 1917 it was still considered a glorious moment for the socialist movement. If Soviet power lasted even just a few days, it would confer great prestige on the Bolshevik revolutionaries and would represent a symbol that could, at some future time, animate the whole international socialist movement.

In addition, by the autumn of 1917, Lenin realized that the revolutionary movement in Russia had started to decline and risked either turning into anarchy or simply disintegrating. In October several Bolshevik leaders felt that they were losing control over the local soviets. At the Central Committee on 23 October, Lenin spoke explicitly of "absenteeism and the indifference of the masses."[4] In the following days, other Bolshevik leaders presented alarming reports. On 29 October, Sverdlov stated that in Petrograd the anarchists were gaining strength in the Putilov factories and the Rozdestvensky district. Skrypnik, who represented the factory workers' committees, asserted that the greater influence of anarchism was being felt everywhere, especially in the Narva area and around Moscow. Schliapnikov announced

---

* The dates of Russian events for the year 1917 are indicated according to the calendar employed outside Russia.

that it was in the metalworkers' union, rather than among the bourgeoisie, that a Bolshevik uprising would be unpopular: "Rumors about it had even caused some panic."[5] The risk existed that Lenin's party might be losing support, while the anarchists and the moderate factions gained in popularity.

The general situation seemed to be evolving unfavorably for the Bolsheviks. Signs indicated that the army might abandon Petrograd to the Germans. The counter-revolutionary generals might try another coup d'état (after the one that had failed in July), overthrowing the provisional government and outlawing the soviets and the revolutionary parties. During the last few days of October and the first few days of November it appeared to Lenin that insurrection and seizure of power were an opportunity not to be missed. Such a move should be made to guarantee the survival of Bolshevism as well as of all Russian socialism. In collective life, just as in the life of individuals, it is the choices necessary for survival that always prevail. As Trotsky wrote about the Bolshevik revolution, "people do not make revolution eagerly any more than they do war. . . . A revolution takes place only when there is no other way out."[6]

Lenin decided to take power whether or not there existed the immediate conditions for widespread revolution. The proletariat of Europe and the rest of the world witnessed the success of the Bolsheviks from the sidelines, without rising up in support. Even in Italy, where the Socialist party had not favored entering the First World War, and where in those days of November the Italian troops were defeated by the Austrians at Caporetto, the "home front" not only did not collapse but somehow gained strength.[7]

From Germany came the news that the leaders of the Social Democratic party, Friedrich Ebert and Philipp Scheidemann, would strongly oppose any demonstrations or strikes in support of the Russian revolutionary movement. They had decided to remain faithful to their government, not to knife it in the back. In fact, there were no revolutionary uprisings in Germany.[8] The German army did not catch the Russian contagion either; it remained faithful to its generals. Lenin's newly formed government then appealed to all the warring countries to make peace, without annexations or war indemnities, but these appeals fell on deaf ears.

Among the Bolsheviks, the party ranks had thought the problem of the war would be solved by a general armistice and world revolution. To have to make separate peace with Germany, Austria, and Turkey meant compromising with imperialists, betraying the proletariat of the world, hindering revolution in Germany, and abandoning hopes of immediate global revolution. On the other hand, how could the Soviets continue to wage war against Germany, a country so much stronger than Russia? Lenin realized that a separate peace had to be signed. The Bolshevik party had been able to seize power because, among other promises, it had vowed to bring peace, and the Russian people were now expecting that promise to be kept. French diplomat Louis de Robien, who was in Petrograd during the days of the Bolshevik takeover, wrote in his diary that by 18 November the population of the capital city was already accusing the Bolsheviks of not having ended the war.[9] Three days later, the soviet of the armed forces hurled the same accusal at Lenin and Trotsky.[10]

The Bolsheviks once again found themselves in a *cul de sac*. If they continued making war, they seriously risked losing their hold on power a few days after having taken over. They had to face two equally dangerous threats: the German cannons on one side and the no-less-fatal risk of popular revolt on the other. This was the dramatic context in which their choice of policy had to be made — certainly a situation that was decidedly different from what they had envisioned in their proclamations.

While Lenin continued to launch appeals for peace, he took a concrete step toward a solution that would rescue Bolshevik power. He proposed the immediate opening of peace negotiations with the Central Powers; and his proposal was accepted. A cease-fire was ordered and negotiations began on 3 December 1917, at Brest-Litovsk. But the ranks of the Bolsheviks and most of their leaders, including Trotsky, went along with Lenin's proposal only because they persisted in the illusion that the negotiations were not going to lead to a separate peace. Instead, they were a way of gaining time in the expectation of revolution in Europe, which they still believed was imminent. Lenin suffered from no such illusions. From the start he realized the many advantages that a separate peace would bring to Bolshevism.

The delegates from Moscow to Brest-Litovsk expressed the same hesitations as the ranks of party members. They did their best to prolong the talks, hoping for the outbreak of revolution in Germany, or at least strikes and uprisings that would free internationalist Russia from having to bow to the imperialists. Trotsky was the head of the delegation to Brest from December 1917 until February 1918, and he refused up to the last moment to sign "a dishonorable peace" treaty. Until the end he persisted in the belief that the Bolsheviks had found a way out in the formula "neither peace nor war," meaning that the armistice was to go on indefinitely.[11]

Lenin was not about to deceive himself, however, and although he was practically isolated, he did not lose his calm determination. Few of the Bolsheviks intended to compromise with the capitalist world, but Lenin was not afraid to stand alone against almost everyone. Minutes of the Central Committee meetings prove that until the end the head of Bolshevism remained in the minority. Therefore, a clear distinction existed between Lenin's ideas and the ideas of the other members of his party, including most of the leaders.

On 8 January, during an assembly of party cadres, Lenin defended the idea of a separate peace. In answer to those opposed to it, who claimed that such a peace would reinforce Austro-German imperialism, Lenin argued that Russia's participation in the war would strengthen Anglo-French imperialism. "In neither case," he observed, "would we be entirely escaping some sort of imperialist bond." With such a premise, the head of the Bolsheviks came to a conclusion which contained the theory of socialism in only one country:

> The correct conclusion from this is that the moment a socialist government triumphed in any one country, questions must be decided, not from the point of view of whether this or that imperialism is preferable, but exclusively from the point of view of the conditions which best make for the development and consolidation of the socialist revolution which has already begun.
>
> In other words, the underlying principle of our tactics must not be, which of the two imperialisms it is more profitable to aid at this juncture, but rather, how the socialist revolution can be most firmly and reliably ensured the possibility of consolidating itself, or, at least, of maintaining itself in one country until it is joined by other countries.[12]

During the following days, Lenin was repeatedly criticized in the Central Committee meetings for his "nationalistic" tendencies. At the 24 January session in particular, Moisey Uritsky declared that Lenin's error lay in his way of considering things "from Russia's point of view rather than from an international one." Tracing the origins of this error, Uritsky remembered that Lenin had revealed dangerous "nationalist" tendencies as far back as 1915–16 in his disputes with Trotsky and others.[13] It was after these disputes that Trotsky had the foreboding of a "Messianic-nationalist-revolutionary attitude" in Lenin, which later led to the dogma of the "Leader State."[14]

On 24 January, most members of the Central Committee were against Lenin. Perhaps they realized that signing a pact with the Germans would preserve Soviet power, but would cause the whole process of revolution to degenerate. The head of the secret police, Dzerzhinsky, stated that signing such an accord was equivalent to "capitulating on the whole program." Bukharin, then editor-in-chief of *Pravda*, put the terms of the dilemma in these words: "Saving our socialist republic, we lose the possibility of success for the international movement." A fall from power might have seemed to Bukharin a solution preferable to betrayal.[15]

Stalin sided with Lenin, as befitted a politician who, like Lenin, was rigorously pragmatic. "No revolutionary movement exists in the West," he declared to the Central Committee on 24 January, "There are no facts to indicate one; there is only a potential, and we cannot count on a potential. . . . In October we spoke of a *holy war*, because they had told us that the word *peace* alone would have provoked revolution in the West. But that didn't happen."[16] Trotsky ended up placing himself in an intermediate position between the pragmatism of Lenin and Stalin and the idealism of Bukharin. On 18 February, it was Trotsky's vote that gave Lenin the majority, enabling him to win final approval of the separate peace.

As the weeks passed, the inevitability of such a peace became increasingly clear. On 10 February, the Brest-Litovsk negotiations had broken off and the German forces had gone back to fighting. By 18 February, the Germans had conquered Dvinsk without even firing a shot, and they crossed the Dvina River on bridges that had been left intact by the withdrawing Soviet troops. The Soviet Supreme Command informed its government that the Red Army was in desperate straits.[17] In the face of the enemy's advance, Lenin abandoned Petrograd and moved the capital to Moscow.

At Brest-Litovsk, on 3 March, the Soviets signed a peace treaty that imposed extremely harsh terms on them. They lost an immense amount of territory — the Ukraine, Poland, part of White Russia, Finland, and the Baltic nations — which was equal to one-quarter of the ex-czarist empire and was inhabited by about 60 million people. The areas they gave up included one-third of the railroad system, more than half the industrial firms, three-quarters of the steel mills, and almost all the coal mines. The dramatic circumstances surrounding this separate peace split the Bolshevik party in two and revived debate on the fundamental principles of the revolution itself, while jeopardizing its development. As Lenin himself confessed on 24 January, in making a separate peace "we are making a turn to the right that will force us to pass through a very dirty barn, but we have to do it."[18]

The majority of the Bolsheviks did not want to pass through the dirty barn. They thought the exercise of power could be accomplished cleanly. On the contrary, Lenin, head of the new government, had to argue from "reasons of state." He saw that the masses, the party ranks, and even the members of the Central Committee found it difficult to bend to the needs of such cold reason. He learned a lesson that he would remember in the future. He understood how necessary it was to watch his words, conceal his thoughts, and not object too drastically to other people's illusions. And yet,

The Brest-Litovsk Accord

on 7 March 1918, when he spoke to the mere thirty-four delegates at the Seventh Party Congress, Lenin wanted to be frank about the unlikelihood of global revolution:

> The revolution will not come as quickly as we expected. History has proved this, and we must be able to take this as a fact, to reckon with the fact that the world socialist revolution cannot begin so easily in the advanced countries as the revolution began in Russia — in the land of Nicholas and Rasputin, in the land in which an enormous part of the population was absolutely indifferent as to what peoples were living in the outlying regions, or what was happening there. In such a country it was quite easy to start a revolution, as easy as lifting a feather.[19]

It was not at all easy to start a revolution in industrialized capitalist countries, where "a democratic culture and method of organization" existed. The peoples of these countries worried about what was happening on the other side of their borders and about the reactions any revolutionary actions of theirs might provoke in the outside world. The Bolsheviks had to accept their diversity and be prepared to wait. They had to learn to be adaptable:

> If you are unable to adapt yourself, if you are not inclined to crawl on your belly in the mud, you are not a revolutionary but a chatterbox; and I propose this not because I like it, but because we have no other road, because history has not been kind enough to bring the revolution to maturity everywhere simultaneously.[20]

The lesson in realism that Lenin taught his comrades — be adaptable and wait — was hard for them to accept. Listening to his words, many of them asked themselves whether the very idea of world revolution was not going to remain forever a dream:

> Yes, we shall see the world revolution, but for the time being it is a very good fairy-tale, a very beautiful fairy-tale — I quite understand children liking beautiful fairy-tales. But I ask, is it proper for a serious revolutionary to believe in fairy-tales?[21]

2
Lenin Aided by the Kaiser

The German government had been secretly financing Russian revolutionary movements since 1915, in order to "destabilize" the czarist empire and force the Czar to sue for peace. To this purpose, in March–April 1917 the government of Germany helped Lenin and other Bolshevik leaders residing in Switzerland to return to their native country. Although they were citizens of an enemy state, the Bolsheviks were authorized to cross through Germany in a special train (which, contrary to what is commonly believed, was not at all "sealed").[1]

The person who planned the unusual and rather reckless scheme, involving an agreement between revolutionaries and imperialists, was a socialist of Russian origin, Alexander Israel Helphand, better known by his pseudonym, Parvus. A few years ago, two Western historians, Zeman and Scharlau, wrote a detailed biography of this "merchant of revolution."[2] Back in 1904, Parvus together with Trotsky had formulated the theory of permanent revolution, and during the ill-fated Russian uprisings of 1905, he was one of the leaders of the St. Petersburg soviet. Arrested in December of that year and deported to Siberia, he managed to escape to Turkey. At the beginning of the First World War, he was once again trying to become one of history's protagonists, and this time he succeeded, partially, in his intent. For all his defects, Parvus did have considerable political talents. Isaac Deutscher wrote that he was "one of the sharpest and most courageous political minds of his generation."[3]

Parvus had decided to come to an agreement with the Germans in 1914 because they were on the same side as the Russian revolutionaries in the struggle against the czarist empire. In a memorandum dated May 1915 he explained to the Berlin government how the Russian revolutionaries could be useful to Germany; however, he did not reveal to the Germans his entire scheme.[4] Parvus probably felt that in the long run it would be international socialism, not German imperialism, that would have the most to gain from such an arrangement. He thought the revolutionary movement would spread from Russia to Germany, and he himself might become the leader of future Russian and German revolutions. He was, after all, one of the first socialists, if not the very first, to maintain that the Russian revolution would act as a prologue to revolution on a European scale.[5]

There is every reason to believe that the Germans had studied the situation carefully before deciding to assist the revolutionaries, and that the Russians, who like Parvus asked the Germans for assistance, had done the same. Each side was trying to use the other to its own advantage, and both sides ran a risk for having secretly come to an agreement. As often occurs in agreements, the objectives of each side were in part the same and in part very different. In this case, the common aim was to create chaos in Russia. The differences would become clear once the chaos had been created.

Lenin knew of the accords that Parvus had come to with the Berlin government. But he was extremely diffident toward Parvus, if not outright hostile, because of old grudges. Moreover, the arrangement between Parvus and Berlin must have seemed to Lenin dangerous for a number of reasons. First, if the German financial assistance should ever come to light, the Russian revolutionaries who had dealt with them would be arrested, tried, and found guilty of conspiring with the enemy. Second, if Parvus, with the help of these financial means, should succeed in penetrating the clandestine Bolshevik organization, he might be able to outmaneuver Lenin and take his place as its leader.

In May 1915, when Parvus went to Zurich to meet with Lenin and tell him many of his plans, Lenin denied him the backing of the Bolshevik party, although he realized that what Parvus was doing was too important to be ignored.[6] Parvus had set up an import-export company in Scandinavia in order to transfer the funds from the Germans into Russia. Lenin decided that some very able and trustworthy Bolshevik should become part of this organization "on a personal basis." Jacob Fuerstenberg, better known by the pseudonym Hanecki, was his man.[7] Hanecki moved to Scandinavia that year to work with Parvus, to keep him in check, and, perhaps later, to use his organization in whatever way Lenin considered opportune.

Lenin's *Collected Works* prove how important Hanecki became in 1917. In March of that year, when Lenin made the decision to return to Russia as soon as possible, he turned to Hanecki, who suggested his traveling through Germany under the authorization of the German government. Until almost the end of the month, Lenin was still very worried about the idea, not wanting to seem in any way a German agent. "Berlin variant is unacceptable to me," he wired Hanecki on 28 March.[8] But as the hours turned into days, Lenin's scruples began to fade. Events were coming to a head in Russia, and to get to Petrograd, he was willing to risk seeming to be backed by the Germans. The Bolsheviks might have the extraordinary opportunity of taking power, and such a grandiose end would justify any means. Lenin decided to travel through Germany as Hanecki had proposed.

Documents discovered only a few years ago in the archives of the German Ministry of Foreign Affairs demonstrate the great care taken, even the fervor shown, by the Berlin authorities in organizing Lenin's journey. The German government along with the Supreme Command and members of the diplomatic corps were mobilized to ensure that the repatriation of Lenin and the other Bolshevik leaders residing in Switzerland would go smoothly. Berlin's Foreign Ministry appealed to Stockholm to facilitate the passage of the Bolsheviks through neutral Sweden. The most zealous person of all in arranging the trip was the Kaiser himself. On 12 April, Wilhelm II made it known that, if Sweden were to deny transit, Lenin and his party would have to return to Russia directly through the frontlines, crossing over the German trenches.[9]

Lenin, meanwhile, was requesting help from Hanecki in Scandinavia, both to organize the passage through Germany and to send money and directives from Sweden to the Bolsheviks in Petrograd. The money, coming as it did from Parvus's organization, had to be from the Germans. "Don't grudge money on communications between Stockholm and Petrograd!", Lenin requested on 30 March.[10] And he specifically asked Hanecki for traveling money for himself and his group: "Earmark 2,000, better 3,000, [Swedish] kronen for our journey."[11] The money arrived and Lenin reassuringly wrote his friend Inessa Armand: "We have more money for the journey than I thought, enough for 10–12 persons. The comrades in Stockholm have been a *great* help."[12]

As soon as he arrived in Sweden, Lenin greeted Hanecki warmly, but he refused to meet with Parvus. Acting as cautiously as possible, he wanted Hanecki, Karl Radek, and the other comrades present to attest in writing to his refusal.[13] All this caution, though, was not enough to prevent deep suspicion from circulating in Russia regarding the relationship between Lenin and the Germans. In April 1917, just after his return to Petrograd, Lenin informed Hanecki and Radek that vehement accusations were already being made: "The bourgeoisie (+ Plekhanov) are furiously attacking us for travelling through Germany. They are trying to incite the soldiers against us. So far it isn't coming off: there are supporters, and loyal ones, among them." In the same letter he again asked for financial aid: "Up to now we have received nothing, absolutely nothing from you — no letters, no packets, no money."[14] But then some money arrived, as Lenin wrote in another letter to the faithful Hanecki: "The money from Kozlowski (2 thous.) has been received."[15]

The men chosen by Lenin to ensure the transfer of funds — Hanecki, Radek, and Kozlowski — were not Russians, they were Poles; and his having chosen non-Russian comrades was further evidence of his efforts at caution. He was well aware of the dangers inherent in the sensitive operation. "Be very regular and careful in your contacts," he continued to remind Hanecki and Radek.[16] Lenin was right to worry. The day after the failed uprising of July 1917, the Petrograd newspapers reported that they had proof Lenin had received money from the Germans, with Hanecki as intermediary. The revelations made "a really enormous impression" on public opinion and forced Lenin to flee and to remain in hiding until the insurrection of 7 November.[17]

From clandestinity, the head of the Bolsheviks tried to reject the charges but he was embarrassed by them. It was difficult to deny what had actually taken place. In his *Collected Works* there is written proof that money passed from Hanecki and Kozlowski to Lenin, and yet in the same source, there are writings in which he desperately tried to deny the obvious. "The Bolsheviks never received *any money* from either Hanecki or Kozlowski," he declared in 1917. "All that is a lie, a complete, vulgar lie."[18] During the summer of 1917, Russian court investigations found that Hanecki had transferred hundreds of thousands of rubles into Russia. Lenin answered these charges by claiming he had never had anything to do with the man: "The Prosecutor's argument is that Parvus is connected with Hanecki, and that Hanecki is connected with Lenin! But this is just a big swindle, for everyone knows that Hanecki had financial dealings with Parvus, but none with me."[19]

A few months later, after Lenin had seized power, he found himself forced to take up the sensitive matter once again. This time, though, it was not in answer to court investigations or bourgeois newspapers (which had been permanently silenced). It was in reaction to an act of his own party's Central Committee. In December 1917, in fact, the Bolshevik Central Committee had decided not to appoint Hanecki as the Soviet representative in Stockholm because he had been part of Parvus's organization. Evidently, many Central Committee members did not know all the details of the affair, or if they did, they intended to distance their responsibility from Hanecki's (and perhaps also Lenin's). On the other hand, Lenin, who knew all the secrets and who interpreted the attacks directed at Hanecki as veiled attacks against himself, retorted furiously:

Hanecki earned his living as an *employee* in a commercial firm of which

Parvus was a shareholder. That is what Hanecki told me. It has not been refuted.

Is it forbidden to work in capitalist commercial undertakings? Where? By what decision of the Party?

Are there no people among us who work in commercial firms of *Russian*, British and other capitalists?

Or is it permissible to be a technician, a manager or an employee of *Russian* capitalists, but not of *German*, even when living in a neutral country?? And is that to be the decision of an "internationalist" party?? . . .

Such a treatment of an absent comrade, who has worked for more than ten years, is the height of *injustice*.[20]

As long as he lived, Lenin remembered his indebtedness to Hanecki and demonstrated how grateful he was. When the first purges of the Bolshevik party took place, Lenin spoke out personally in Hanecki's favor.[21] And when the time came to find a comrade who was worthy of being the head of the Soviet State Bank, he chose Hanecki. After all, Lenin had had the opportunity to appreciate what a gifted financier the man was.[22]

There are also German sources that document to what extent the funds from Berlin contributed to Lenin's success. In a message of 29 September 1917, German Foreign Minister Richard von Kühlmann made it very clear when he wrote: "The Bolshevik movement could never have attained the scale or influence which it has today without our continual support."[23] Then, in a message on 3 December, he re-stated Germany's political intentions and noted how substantial the aid sent to Lenin had been. The Berlin government credited itself with the success of Bolshevik propaganda and its official newspaper, *Pravda*:

> Russia appeared to be the weakest link in the enemy chain. The task therefore was gradually to loosen it, and, when possible, to remove it. This was the purpose of the subversive activity we caused to be carried out in Russia behind the front — in the first place promotion of separatist tendencies and support of the Bolsheviks. It was not until the Bolsheviks had received from us steady flow of funds through various channels and under different labels that they were in a position to be able to build up their main organ, *Pravda*, to conduct energetic propaganda and appreciably to extend the originally narrow basis of their party.[24]

Therefore, it was not surprising that Germany took care to finance the Bolsheviks even after they came to power. Diego von Bergen, in charge of Russian affairs for Berlin's Foreign Ministry, wired the German Legation in

Bern on 28 November 1917: "According to information received here, the government in Petrograd is having to fight against great financial difficulties. It is therefore very desirable that they be sent money."[25] The Germans realized that the survival of Soviet power was in their own best interests.

3

The German Bourgeoisie's Preference for the Bolsheviks

Until the autumn of 1918, the Germans continued to dominate the scene in Russia through their daring policy toward the Bolsheviks and the presence of their army, which was capable of backing that policy. The Entente powers held a secondary role. They lacked both a clear policy and the armed forces to support it. The Allies did carry on circumscribed military actions, such as landings at several ports of the ex-czarist empire, but on the whole their commitment was quite limited. In the spring of 1918, the French and the English had suffered heavy losses in Picardy, in Flanders, and at the Chemin des Dames, and they certainly were in no condition to divert any more forces to Russia. The Italians, who had suffered a severe defeat at Caporetto, were trying to reorganize their army. The Americans were arriving at the French front in goodly numbers, but they could not deploy many troops on other fronts.[1]

Only the Japanese, who landed at Vladivostok in April 1918, were able to deploy substantial forces against the Bolsheviks. But in May Lenin declared that the Germans continued to be a greater threat than the Japanese. As he told the Central Committee, "war against Germany threatens greater losses and calamities than against Japan."[2] His conviction was that the Soviets had to go on negotiating with the Germans. Trotsky resigned as Foreign Commissar in March 1918 because, during the Brest-Litovsk negotiations, acting as spokesman for a policy that was decidedly different from Lenin's, he had argued violently with the Germans. In his memoirs, Trotsky said his resignation was designed to facilitate the talks.[3]

Trotsky's replacement was Georgy V. Chicherin, a talented diplomat who directed Soviet foreign policy until 1930. Chicherin was one of Lenin's most faithful aides. It was not unusual for him to be called upon more than once during a day to consult with the leader. The Russian-born Chicherin, who was 46 years old in 1918, was of Italian origin — the family's original name, Ciceroni, had been suitably Russianized. As a young man, before he became a socialist and was forced to emigrate, he had worked as a civil servant in the archives of the Ministry of Foreign Affairs under the czarist regime. A man of vast culture, he was fluent in five languages. According to American historian Louis Fischer, who knew him well, "Chicherin was a genius" with "intensity of perception, imagination and intuition."[4] He was the one who, along with Lenin, gave concrete form to the policy of cooperation with Germany that characterized the months following the Brest-Litovsk agreement — a policy that would have been greatly hindered by Trotsky's continued presence at the Foreign Ministry.

The pro-German line was a confirmation of the extremely pragmatic approach taken by Lenin in foreign policy and his desire, above all, to guarantee the survival of the Bolshevik state through the establishment of normal relations with other nations. The governments of Moscow and Berlin were both convinced from the start that it was possible to come to a broad agreement. A document dated November 1917 testifies once again to how profoundly interested the Kaiser was in Russian affairs. On 27 November, the Germans and the Bolsheviks had decided to meet in Brest to negotiate a separate peace, and two days later Wilhelm II sent a communiqué to his Foreign Minister, saying: "In spite of everything" try to reach "some kind of alliance or friendly relations with the Russians." The Kaiser went on to say he had already told his Supreme Command that it was opportune to help the Russians get the railroads working again as soon as possible. He added that in the future he hoped "to set up a close commercial relationship with the Russians."[5]

A few days later, as the negotiations were getting under way, Foreign Minister von Kühlmann communicated to Wilhelm II that a separate peace would promote the desired *rapprochement* between Russia and Germany:

> The conclusion of a separate peace would mean the achievement of the desired war aim, namely a breach between Russia and her Allies. The amount of tension necessarily caused by such a breach would determine the degree of Russia's dependence on Germany and her future relations with us. Once cast out and cast off by her former Allies, abandoned financially, Russia will be forced to seek our support. We shall be able to provide help for Russia in various ways; firstly in the rehabilitation of the railways (I have in mind a German Russian Commission, under our control, which would undertake the rational and coordinated exploitation of the railway lines so as to ensure speedy resumption of freight move-

ment); then the provision of a substantial loan, which Russia requires to maintain her state machine. This could take the form of an advance on security of grain, raw materials, etc., to be provided by Russia and shipped under the control of the above mentioned commission. Aid on such a basis — the scope to be increased as and when necessary — would in my opinion bring about a growing *rapprochement* between the two countries.

Von Kühlmann added that the head of the Foreign Ministry of the Austro-Hungarian Empire, Count Czernin, was even more anxious than the Germans to reach a stable accord with Moscow, and he explained why:

I would interpret the excessive eagerness of Count Czernin to come to terms with the Russians as a desire to forestall us and to prevent Germany and Russia arriving at an intimate relationship inconvenient to the Danube Monarchy. There is no need for us to compete for Russia's good will. We are strong enough to wait with equanimity; we are in a far better position than Austria-Hungary to offer Russia what she needs for the reconstruction of her state.[6]

The following day the Kaiser confirmed to his minister that he was favorable to a Russian-German *rapprochement*.[7] And a few days after, on 16 December, the Supreme Commander, General Ludendorff, declared himself in favor of an alliance with Russia.[8]

The tensions that were building up during the talks in Brest were due to Trotsky, along with most of the members of the Bolshevik party — certainly not to Lenin. For a time it seemed that the Russian-German reconciliation might not take place. Once the peace treaty was signed, however, the atmosphere quickly changed for the better. By the second half of April 1918, Germany and Soviet Russia were already exchanging ambassadors. The Germans named Count Wilhelm von Mirbach-Harff as ambassador to Moscow and the Russians sent a 35-year-old revolutionary, Adolf Abramovich Ioffe, as ambassador to Berlin. A member of the Central Committee, Ioffe came from a rich family, had been imprisoned under the Czar, and had joined the Bolshevik party in August 1917, together with Trotsky.

One might well wonder whether Berlin had in mind a *rapprochement* with Bolshevik Russia or with a different Russia. But the German documents dated May 1918 put all doubts to rest. The reconciliation was definitely to be with the Bolsheviks themselves. The German Ambassador was quite explicit in a telegram sent from Moscow on 13 May: "It appears to me, as I see from here, that our interests still demand the continuation in power of the Bolshevik government." It was his opinion that any other Russian government would have demanded a revision of the Brest-Litovsk treaty, and such an occurrence was to be carefully avoided. Therefore, it was best to continue supplying the Bolsheviks with the goods indispensable to them and to do all possible to keep them in power.[9]

Von Mirbach reported on 16 May that the Entente powers were spending considerable sums of money to bring about the fall of Lenin's government. "I am still trying to counter efforts of the Entente and support the Bolsheviks," the Ambassador telegraphed, asking his government for further instructions. Foreign Minister von Kühlmann replied immediately: "Please use larger sums, as it is greatly in our interests that Bolsheviks should survive."[10]

Naturally, not everyone in Germany was so pro-Bolshevik. The Supreme Command, especially, did not trust Lenin and was secretly dealing with the anti-Bolsheviks.[11] But those in favor of Lenin prevailed. Besides the Kaiser and most of the political figures, the economic forces of the country also looked favorably on the new Russia. On that same 16 May, a group of big German industrialists, among them Krupp, Stinnes, and Thyssen, delivered a memorandum to their government. In it the industrial magnates predicted that at the end of the war economic conflicts would break out among the great powers. They were afraid the German state would not be able to win back all its pre-war markets; however, the enormous Russian market could be won, they felt, and the country could supply many natural resources as well. The industrialists wanted to set up a consortium to promote Russian-German trade, with a capital investment of two billion marks, and they asked the government to help ensure the success of the undertaking.[12] Their wishes were that the Russian-German agreement not be a limited affair, made necessary by the dictates of war. It was, instead, to be an economic and political operation of great scope, leading to a new world order once the war had ended.

According to Soviet documents, Lenin was informed immediately of the prevailing pro-Bolshevik tendency in Germany. Ambassador Ioffe, just after his arrival in Berlin, sent a communiqué stating that the major German banks and industrial firms were opposed to continuing hostilities and wanted to establish commercial relations with Russia.[13] Lenin was delighted with the news, and on 10 May he took up the issue with the Central Committee. He declared that German leaders were split on the question of Russia and that, although there was an extremist faction which wanted to make war on the Bolsheviks, this group was in the minority:

> It is an undoubted fact that the majority of the imperialist bourgeoisie in Germany are against such a policy and at the present moment prefer the annexationist peace with Russia to a continuation of the war for the simple reason that war would divert forces from the West and increase the

instability of the internal situation in Germany that is already making itself felt; it would also make it difficult to obtain raw materials from places involved in insurrection or that are suffering from damage to railways, from failure to plant sufficient crops, etc., etc.[14]

The Central Committee gave official approval to Lenin's position on 13 May, and Foreign Commissar Chicherin radioed a message to Berlin proposing broad negotiations that would include all the major questions existing between Russia and Germany.[15] Two days later, under Lenin's instructions, the Commercial Commissar, M. G. Bronski, took a significant step by meeting with Ambassador von Mirbach and making a series of proposals to foster a great increase in trade relations. The Bolsheviks offered raw materials and authorized "concessions" to German companies for the exploitation of Russian mineral resources and forest products. In exchange they requested the loan of various industrial products and the technical assistance needed to reconstruct their railways and modernize their agriculture. They wanted assurances, furthermore, that the Germans would in no way interfere in Soviet economic policy.[16]

On 19 May, the Kaiser ordered his army to abstain from all military operations on Russian soil, and the next day, Foreign Minister von Kühlmann informed the Bolsheviks that Germany was ready to open negotiations for a wide-ranging agreement.[17]

4

The Berlin Treaties

Lenin considered the negotiations that were about to begin in Berlin of utmost importance; he felt sure they would quickly lead to positive results. Meanwhile, few good things were happening for the new-born Soviet state. The power of the Bolsheviks in May 1918 was both limited and tenuous. The ex-czarist empire had broken up; the Germans had come into possession of vast regions in the west, including the Ukraine and the Crimea; the Turks had advanced into the region of the Caucasus, and the British had occupied several ports on the White Sea. Furthermore, that same month thousands of Czechoslovak ex-prisoners rebelled against the Soviets, joining other counter-revolutionary forces and giving rise to civil war. The Red Army was incapable of an adequate military response. As historian W.H. Chamberlin has written, "within a few weeks an enormous territory was wrested from Soviet control."[1] The economic situation was even worse than the military one. The official history of the Russian Communist party, published in 1938, states that in 1918:

> There was a shortage of bread and meat. The workers were starving. In Moscow and Petrograd a bread ration of one-eighth of a pound was issued to them every other day, and there were times when no bread was issued at all. The factories were at a standstill, owing to a lack of raw materials and fuel.[2]

Discouragement and desperation were widespread among the communists. On 4 June, Lenin himself said: "For it is a fact that when they sensed the tremendous difficulties that confront us in the revolution, many members of the working masses gave way to despair."[3] This general picture helps to explain why Lenin conducted the Berlin negotiations as he did. Soviet power was very fragile and needed German support even more than before.

Lenin sent Ambassador Ioffe a personal message on 2 June 1918, in which he explained that the Soviet delegation to the Berlin talks would be made up of other leading party members besides Ioffe himself, including Sokolnikov, Bukharin, Larin, Krasin, and, last but not least, Hanecki.[4] Sokolnikov was an old acquaintance of the Germans, since he had headed the Bolshevik delegation at Brest-Litovsk on the very day the peace treaty was signed. Bukharin was the one who had most strongly opposed the treaty. For him, becoming part of the delegation to Berlin meant a further admission of defeat. Larin, a former Menshevik, was an expert in economic matters, and Krasin, an engineer, once worked for the German company Siemens and Schuckert. Hanecki needs no introduction, of course.

It is noteworthy that Lenin, in his personal message of 2 June, suggested that Ambassador Ioffe be wary of all the members of the Bolshevik delegation except Krasin and Hanecki:

> Bukharin acts in good faith, but he is up to the neck in "Left stupidness." Sokolnikov has gone astray again. Larin is a floundering intellectual, a first-class bungler. Therefore be extremely on your guard with all these most charming, most admirable delegates. Sokolnikov is a very valuable worker, but sometimes (as just now) something "comes over him" and he "breaks china" because of paradoxes. If you do not take precautions, he will break china there with you. And Bukharin — triply so. *Prenez garde*! I hope that Krasin and Hanecki, being business-like people, will help you and the whole matter will be smoothed out.

This rather scornfully worded message, instructing Ioffe to be diffident toward Sokolnikov, Bukharin, and Larin, shows how isolated Lenin felt when it came to foreign policy. It also means that at that time only a few of the Bolsheviks — the "practical" and open-minded ones — correctly interpreted their leader's directives. Actually, Hanecki did not go to Berlin, probably because he still had many enemies on the Central Committee, and Lenin had to give in to their preferences.[5] Only Krasin, among the "practical" men, remained part of the Bolshevik delegation.

Lenin also gave Ioffe certain basic instructions in the 2 June message. The Germans were to understand the advantages they would gain from an agreement and the disadvantages of a resumption of fighting: "If the German traders will accept economic advantages, realizing that *nothing* is to be got from us by war, for we shall burn *everything* — then our policy will continue to be successful. We can give the Germans raw materials." But it was not necessary to threaten the German government. Berlin was perhaps even more ready than Moscow to make an agreement.

The preliminary talks between the Soviet Ambassador and the Minister of Foreign Affairs, von Kühlmann, began in the German capital on 29 June 1918. Discussions opened with political and military topics that went well beyond the commercial questions. In fact, at those preliminary meetings the issue of Russian-German collaboration in the Caucasus was taken up, since the Turkish army was threatening the oil wells of Baku. The Germans promised that their Turkish allies would not get as far as the wells. In exchange they asked the Russians to supply them with petroleum. This pleased Lenin, who informed Stalin of the success of his diplomacy.[6]

How great the desire was to reach an accord emerged with what happened, or rather what did not happen, when the German Ambassador was assassinated in Moscow. On 6 July, two members of the political police, Iakov Bliumkin and Nikolay Andreyev, entered the German embassy and murdered Count Mirbach. Bliumkin and Andreyev were agents for the Left Socialist Revolutionaries, and their action was part of a conspiracy whose aim was to overthrow Lenin's government. The Left Socialist Revolutionaries had decided to kill Ambassador von Mirbach because they realized that, at that moment, the major element of support for Bolshevism was Germany. They hoped that the assassination would mean the end of this support, a break-off of Russian-German relations, and perhaps even a resumption of military hostilities.[7]

The hopes of the conspirators never came to pass. The German leaders laid the blame on the plotters themselves and on the secret services of the Entente powers, not on Lenin. The Russian-German negotiations in Berlin had gotten underway in such a friendly atmosphere, and they corresponded so perfectly to the Bolshevik "reasons of state," that it made no sense to attribute to Lenin any intention of endangering the outcome. Immediately after receiving the news of von Mirbach's death, Lenin had, in fact, hurried to the German embassy to offer his condolences in person. He had expressed his dismay over the crime and solemnly repeated his desire for peace. The leaders in Berlin had no reason to doubt him. Even the Kaiser voiced his disagreement with those who proposed recalling the diplomatic staff from Moscow. "Right now," he said, "we have to support the Bolsheviks under any circumstances."[8]

Not even the replacement of the German Minister of Foreign Affairs (Admiral Paul von Hintze took von Kühlmann's post) on 9 July had any effect on Berlin's policy toward Moscow. The Russian-German talks proceeded and von Hintze named Karl Helfferich, ex-Vice Chancellor of the Reich and well-known economist, the new Ambassador to Moscow. Following the assassination of von Mirbach, the Bolsheviks authorized the Germans to send a detachment of 300 soldiers to Moscow to protect the new Ambassador and the other diplomats. The Germans, however, never sent their soldiers.[9]

The Bolsheviks then revealed they were willing to receive a much larger contingent of German soldiers. When the forces of the Entente captured Onega (on the White Sea) on 18 August, Chicherin went to the German embassy to request aid. In the name of the Soviet government he asked the Germans to send troops to Russia to fight both the Entente Allies and the White forces. He explicitly stated that the only reason Lenin's government did not make a formal alliance with Germany was that public opinion prevented it. He requested, however, that the German troops refrain from entering Petrograd. Ambassador Helfferich reported the conversation to Berlin and suggested accepting Chicherin's request for troops and then using the same forces against the Bolsheviks. Foreign Minister von Hintze, who had every intention of continuing to cooperate with the Bolsheviks, indignantly rejected the new Ambassador's suggestions. When von Hintze asked his Supreme Commander, General Ludendorff, if his forces were in a position to aid the Bolsheviks, the General declared he was quite ready to send troops to Russia. But Ludendorff opposed Chicherin's request regarding Petrograd, where he would have liked one of the military bases to be. The Foreign Minister disagreed and began having second thoughts about the advisability of sending armed forces. He realized this would mean putting complete control over foreign policy toward Russia into the hands of the military, so he proposed a compromise solution to the Bolsheviks. The Red Army was to pull back its divisions from the line of demarcation agreed on at Brest-Litovsk in order to use them against the Allied forces and the Whites, while the Germans would promise not to take advantage of the situation. That is what was done.[10]

Ambassador Helfferich, meanwhile, was sending wires to Berlin stating that if the Germans withdrew their support, the Bolsheviks would fall from power. Von Hintze agreed completely but, unlike his Ambassador, he was convinced that Germany's best interests would not be served by the collapse of the Bolshevik regime, since any other Russian government would renege on the Brest-Litovsk peace treaty.[11] The German Foreign Minister explained the essentials of his *Realpolitik* to General Ludendorff:

> Whether we like working with [the Bolsheviks] or not is irrelevant, so long as it is useful. History proves that to introduce feelings into politics is an expensive luxury. In our position it would be irresponsible to allow ourselves such a luxury. A man who works with the Bolsheviks as the men de facto in power and then sighs over the nastiness of the company is harmless; but to refuse to benefit from working with the Bolsheviks out of reluctance to incur the odium of having to do with the Bolsheviks — that is dangerous. Politics have always been utilitarian, and will be so for a long time to come.[12]

The Russian-German accords were drawn up in their final form on 10 August, and signed on the 27th of that month in Berlin. According to the agreements, Soviet Russia gave up Estonia and took on the task of ridding Russia's northern regions of Entente military forces. Germany, in return, settled on new borders for the Ukraine that were more favorable to Russia, and promised to evacuate White Russia as soon as the Soviets had paid indemnities amounting to the considerable sum of six billion marks, to be handed over in installments. A secret protocol was also signed in which the Germans made important concessions to the Soviets at the expense of the Ukrainians and the Georgians. They gave the Russians a free hand to fight the Turks in Azerbaijan and Armenia, and they undertook to fight the White forces led by General Alekseev. The Bolshevik government, in turn, accepted the eventuality of German military intervention on Soviet territory if the Red Army did not succeed in driving the Entente forces out of the White Sea and the Caucasus. Clearly, it was a wide-ranging political military agreement.[13]

Historian Louis Fischer has described the Russo-German accords of August 1918 as "much better than Brest. Yet the rapid sinking of the central powers warranted a bigger victory for Moscow."[14] Nonetheless, the Bolsheviks were jubilant, as *Manchester Guardian* correspondent Morgan Philips Price reported in his eye-witness account from Moscow.[15] Foreign Commissar Chicherin, who presented the Russo-German treaties to the Executive Central Committee of the Soviets, declared that they represented a "significant improvement" of the Soviet position in international relations. Of course, he could not make any reference to the further advantages contained in the secret protocol.[16] Meanwhile, at a political rally held for Moscow trade-unionists, Karl Radek explained that after the signing of the accords, Germany had nothing to gain by overthrowing the power of the Soviets.[17] On his part, Lenin commented on 29 July, while the Berlin negotiations were drawing to a close:

> Germany is now negotiating with us as to how many thousand millions to extort from Russia . . . but she has recognized all the acts of nationalization we proclaimed under the decree of June 28th. She has not raised the question of private ownership of land in the republic.

According to him, Germany recognized a certain degree of autonomy for the Soviet state and continued to guarantee its survival: "The fact of the matter is that, burdensome as the peace treaty may be, we have won freedom to carry on socialist construction at home."[18]

The treaties between the Soviet state and the Hohenzollerns — those made public and those kept secret — seemed to consolidate Lenin's power.

But they certainly did nothing for world revolution, and the Russian revolutionaries who were still hoping in it were filled with indignation. This was one of the reasons why an anti-Bolshevik revolutionary named Fanja Kaplan fired three shots at Lenin on 30 August 1918. Two bullets hit him. One fractured his left shoulder; the other pierced his left lung and lodged in his clavicular breast-bone. Though he survived, Lenin's health was never the same again. Fanja Kaplan was put to death four days later.[19]

5

The Hostility between Lenin and Rosa Luxemburg

During the two months that Lenin spent recuperating from his gunshot wounds it became clear that Germany was going to lose the First World War. By November Germany had been defeated and the war was over. The treaties with Berlin, therefore, would no longer be able to guarantee the survival of the Soviet state. It is often said that Lenin was expecting to find this guarantee in the advent of world revolution, but in March 1918 he had already called it a "fairy tale."[1] He certainly had no reason to change his mind in November. On the contrary, the end of the war brought with it a new element of stability, not of disorder. Many years later, Maksim Litvinov, one of the Soviet foreign policymakers, went so far as to assert that the hopes of global revolution ended on the very first day of peace — 11 November 1918.[2]

The fact that Germany was thrown into disorder by revolutionary uprisings at the end of the war might support the theory of world revolution. The Kaiser abdicated on 8 November, the country was declared a republic, and Social Democratic leader Friedrich Ebert became Chancellor of the Reich. In reporting these events, *Pravda* presented them as the start of world revolution, and the ranks of Bolsheviks enthusiastically proclaimed 10 November a national holiday in honor of revolutionary Germany. But while the masses celebrated, Lenin's closest aides noted that he was filled with anxiety. On one of those November days, Karl Radek found himself next to Lenin on the balcony of the Moscow soviet building while he was addressing the crowd. As Radek later wrote, "his face showed excitement and at the same time profound anxiety. I did not understand at that moment why this champion of the revolution was anxious." A few days later, Radek found the answer:

His face was as worried as it had been on the balcony of the Moscow Soviet. "The gravest moment," Lenin explained, "has arrived. Germany is beaten. The Entente's road to Russia is cleared. Even if Germany does not take part in the campaign against us, the hands of the Allies are free."[3]

During the same days, *Manchester Guardian* correspondent Morgan Philips Price met Lenin in the Kremlin and had a similar impression of the leader:

> I was surprised to find that he did not seem to share the prevailing optimism about the imminence of the world revolution. On the contrary, he seemed to think that the events in Central Europe might expose the Soviet republic to new and greater dangers.[4]

Lenin had a decidedly pessimistic resolution passed by the Congress of Soviets on 8 November. It proclaimed there were no longer two groups of imperialist powers capable of annihilating each other. Only one group of winners remained — the Anglo-French imperialists — and they were about to divide up the world and overthrow the Bolsheviks. The resolution went on to say that the masses in Russia were not aware of this terrible danger. It was, therefore, the duty of the Soviets to make them realize that "an attack of forces immeasurably more dangerous" than the Whites was being prepared.[5] Lenin's pessimism was justified because the pre-existing international equilibrium had been destroyed and the situation in Germany had totally changed after the war.

First of all, the Social Democrats who came to power in Germany with the advent of the republic were not as well disposed toward Bolshevism as the Kaiser had been. The country was now under Allied control, and if the Allies proposed an anti-Bolshevik crusade to the Germans offering more favorable terms of peace in return, Berlin might accept the offer. Second, no pro-Bolshevik revolutionary party capable of overthrowing the Social Democrats existed in Germany. Third, the whole German socialist movement had very different characteristics and traditions from Russian Bolshevism. Even Rosa Luxemburg, leader of the leftists closest to Bolshevism, was critical of the Soviet state and opposed to Lenin.

As for the total absence of a pro-Bolshevik policy on the part of the German Social Democrats, on 5 November the government coalition headed by Prince Max von Baden, in which the Social Democrats participated, broke off relations with Soviet Russia and expelled Ambassador Ioffe along with embassy personnel totalling 186 people.[6] On 16 November, Chicherin and Radek had a two-hour exchange of views via teletype from Moscow to Berlin with the leader of the Independent Social Democrats, Hugo Haase, who was a member of Germany's new government. The conversation confirmed that the changes in the international situation had convinced the German republic to abandon the Kaiser's pro-Soviet policy. Haase made it clear that, while in the future the Social Democrats might be willing to resume diplomatic relations with Moscow, for the moment they had no such intentions. He also pointed out that Germany's signing of the armistice was not a stratagem to gain time, but rather the start of real peace negotiations with the Allies.

In order to distance the new German government even further from Moscow, the Russian offer of wheat, made by Chicherin on behalf of his hungry country, was refused. Haase informed the Russians that the United States had already guaranteed the Germans all the grain they would need for the winter.[7] The Bolsheviks considered this refusal a very serious affront. They had already harvested the grain and begun to load it on two trains, at the cost of great sacrifice. The editor in chief of *Izvestiia*, Iury Steklov, voiced their indignation when he wrote that the German Social Democrats had obtained wheat from America because they had promised to protect bourgeois society and because perhaps they had already signed a secret anti-Soviet pact with the Allies.[8]

There is no doubt that the German revolution was carried out in a way that was not at all favorable to the Bolsheviks. On 23 December 1918, Lenin defined Germany's Social Democrats, who had come to power under the republic, as "traitor-socialists."[9] In Germany there did not exist any pro-Bolshevik movement that might have been able to alter the political situation. The Social Democratic government had a solid hold on power; it enjoyed a broad range of popular support and the military leaders backed it — their very purpose being to prevent Bolshevism from spreading to their country.[10]

Bolshevik propaganda of the day claimed that the leader of Germany's Spartacist group, Karl Liebknecht, might still have a chance to take power. But as historian Pierre Broué has put it, Liebknecht was "alone," since the real workers' vanguard was organized by the Independent Social Democratic party, which was run by centrist elements, and Liebknecht was in constant disagreement with it. During a decisive assembly of the Workers' and Soldiers' Councils, on 9 November, Liebknecht realized fully how isolated he was. According to Broué, almost all the soldiers were against him, and they interrupted his speech with catcalls and insults and even threatened him with their weapons. Little more than a month later, when 489 delegates to the First Congress of the Workers' and Soldiers' Councils met, there were only ten Spartacists and eleven United Revolutionaries, and Karl Liebknecht had not even been elected a delegate. It is true that outside the congress hall these same two groups succeeded in attracting great crowds to their rallies, but the results were nil. As Broué has written, by then their position had been compromised.[11]

Though Lenin could not realistically have expected a communist revolution to take place in Germany, he might not even have wanted one. German socialism and Russian Bolshevism were profoundly diverse, and a personal antagonism separated Rosa Luxemburg from Lenin and the Bolsheviks. The difference arose partly from the political, economic, and social conditions existing in the two countries. Germany was a great industrial power, Russia primarily an agricultural country. The German socialists had been openly organizing parties and unions for decades and had participated in parliament. The czarist autocracy had prevented Russian communists from having similar experiences. But another important element of diversity lay in the rigidly hierarchical and centralized manner in which Lenin had organized his party from the year 1903 onward (after he had published *What Is to Be Done*). Germany's socialists found his approach repugnant to their democratic traditions. Rosa Luxemburg had expressed their repugnance in a long article published in *Neue Zeit* in 1904:

> The ultra-centralism that Lenin recommends seems to us to be totally permeated not by a positive and creative spirit but rather by the sterile spirit of a night watchman. His conception is basically directed toward controlling the party's activity rather than making it more fertile; it is motivated by a desire to restrain the movement not to encourage its development, to suffocate it rather than unify it.[12]

Her observations were precise, her remarks penetrating, and they inevitably provoked deep resentment in someone as proud and intolerant as Lenin. She went on:

> To stifle the workers movement in a strait-jacket of bureaucratic centralism that reduces the militant proletariat to a mere tool of a "committee" is the easiest and surest way of handing over the still-young workers movement to power-craving intellectuals.[13]

The Leninist intellectuals were indignant. Lenin sent the *Neue Zeit* a strongly worded reply, but its editor, Karl Kautsky, refused to print it. Lenin accused Rosa Luxemburg of bad faith and stupidity: "Comrade Luxemburg . . . repeats naked words without troubling to grasp their concrete meaning." He considered her criticism of his centralist approach "nothing but a vulgarization of Marxism, a perversion of true Marxian dialectics."[14]

After 1904, there were other contrasts between the two leaders over various issues: the nature of imperialism, the unification of the fractious Russian socialist parties, the question of nationalities. In October 1912, Rosa Luxemburg defined one of Lenin's circulars regarding the Polish party as "the latest in a series of scandals perpetrated by this comrade," and she accused him of "encouraging the divisive ambitions of a factionalism gone mad."[15] She denounced Lenin's Bolsheviks in an article appearing in *Sozialdemokrat* the following year. According to her, after having spent years unscrupulously and methodically bringing about a "split" in the Russian workers movement, the Bolsheviks were trying to repeat the operation in Poland and Lithuania.[16] Lenin's replies were no less rancorous. In 1914, while arguing with her over the nationalities issue, he described an article of hers as "a collection of errors in logic that could be used for schoolboy exercises. . . . sheer nonsense and a mockery of the historically concrete presentation of the question. . . . a collection of empty and meaningless platitudes."[17] During these bitter fights Lenin included Luxemburg on the list of his worst enemies, along with Kautsky, Martov, and Plekhanov.[18]

Rosa Luxemburg's anti-Bolshevism sharpened in 1918, owing to Lenin's policy toward imperialist Germany. She condemned the Brest-Litovsk peace treaty, convinced that it strangled both the Russian and the German revolutions. She witnessed the Russo-German negotiations in Berlin with growing anxiety. By the summer of 1918, as the outlines of a Moscow-Berlin alliance became clear, she referred to it as "a dismal spectre," a catastrophe for world revolution: "An alliance between Bolshevism and German imperialism would be a terrible mortal blow to international socialism, which it would not be able to stand up to."[19]

The situation in Germany that Lenin had to deal with in November 1918 consisted of two main elements: the existence of a solid Social Democratic government which, contrary to its predecessor, was hostile to Moscow, and the existence of a Spartacist movement inimical to the Social Democrats but with a history of fifteen years of hostility toward Russian Bolshevism. This state of affairs was also under examination by the Menshevik movement.

The members of this group came to the conclusion they should back the revolution in Germany and cooperate with German leftists to overthrow Lenin's government. One of the better known Menshevik leaders, Iulii Martov, sent a message to his German comrades in December 1918, stating: "We now look on Berlin and not Moscow as the center of the Revolution. . . . We ask you also to proclaim to the Congress [the Reich Congress of Workers' and Soldiers' Councils] the thought embodied in our resolutions and appeals, that *Germany is today the heart of the proletarian world revolution.*"[20]

The Mensheviks felt that a victorious workers' revolution in a rich, powerful, and industrial nation like Germany would take so much revolutionary prestige away from the Bolsheviks that it would be the beginning of their downfall.

Lenin's evaluation of the events could not have been very different. The leader of the Bolsheviks decided to send Karl Radek to Germany in November 1918, giving him the following instructions on his mission: the revolution in Germany, by diverting the enemy's attention, was to prevent possible attack of Russia by the Entente countries. Radek had some misgivings. "The German revolution," he objected, "is too great an event to be regarded as a diversion in the rear of the enemy." Was it really possible that Lenin considered it nothing more than that? "Yes," Lenin answered, "I don't suggest that you should force developments; they will proceed according to the internal laws of the German revolution." This was how Radek recorded the conversation in a book he published in 1926, but it is very likely that the two men discussed a great deal more in 1918.[21]

It is significant that it was Radek who became the Bolshevik leader's representative to Berlin. If Lenin had intended to settle long-time disagreements with Rosa Luxemburg, to win new friends among Berlin's Social Democrats, and to link the Russian revolution with the German one, he would never have sent Radek. In 1912, when Karl Radek was a member of both the Polish and German Socialist parties, he was expelled from the Polish party on the urging of Luxemburg herself and his name was put up by her for expulsion from the German one, too. He was accused of some very defamatory offenses — stealing money, books, and clothing from party comrades. Luxemburg also suspected that Radek and other Polish comrades, all friends of Lenin (including Jacob Hanecki), were somehow in contact with the German secret police. These accusations and suspicions were rooted in the deep political contrasts between Luxemburg and fellow socialists on one side and the Polish pro-Bolsheviks on the other.[22] During the controversy Lenin had taken Radek's part, in opposition to Rosa Luxemburg. According to him, she was guilty of "intrigues," "malicious bits of gossip," and "petty old wives' tales."[23]

The events of 1912–13 had been too dramatic to be forgotten, and in 1918 Radek and Luxemburg still hated each other. When he arrived clandestinely in Berlin that November she tried to avoid meeting him. But it simply could not be that one of the best minds behind a revolution under way refused to speak to the envoy of a victorious revolution. She was finally convinced to be more flexible. But when the meeting did take place, it was described as "cold and formal."[24]

Radek quickly perceived the general tendencies among the Spartacists. None of them, least of all Luxemburg, intended to force the pace of insurrection. This was reassuring to Lenin's envoy.[25] His worries involved Luxemburg's hostility toward Bolshevism and her intention to remain autonomous. Liebknecht was closer to Lenin's way of thinking, but he was somewhat confused and uncertain.[26] What prevented Luxemburg from making her criticism of Lenin public was the enthusiasm of the Spartacist ranks for the Bolsheviks. Her sharply critical opinions circulated among the Spartacist leaders, however, and had their desired effect on the atmosphere that surrounded Radek.

In 1918 Rosa Luxemburg outlined her views on the Bolsheviks in writing, but the piece was made public only after her death. In it she began by praising Lenin for his merits. Then she went on to attack his agrarian policy and his policy regarding national self-determination for the non-Russian ethnic groups. She protested against the suppression (wanted by the Bolsheviks) of the constituent assembly and against the suppression of democracy in general. She wrote: "If liberty is reserved only for the pro-government elements, for the members of one single party — however numerous they may be — it is not liberty. Liberty always means liberty for those who disagree." She insisted that socialism could not be "decreed or conceded by a dozen intellectuals sitting around a table." She added that Lenin was "completely wrong" when he set up ways of checking on and controlling the people: "Decrees, dictatorial powers for the factory inspectors, draconian punishments, terrorism."[27] Her denouncement was biting and concise:

> Lenin and Trotsky replaced the representative bodies elected by universal suffrage with the soviets, which were to become the only true representation for the working masses. But once political life is suffocated in the whole country, it is inevitable that the soviets themselves become paralyzed. Without general elections, without unlimited liberty of the press and of assembly, without the free circulation of opinion, the life goes out of all public institutions. They just give the appearance of being alive. The only active element becomes the bureaucracy. Public life falls slowly into lethargy.
> A couple of dozen party heads with untiring energy and unlimited idealism manage and govern. Among these, the actual leadership is in the hands of about a dozen superior minds. A chosen elite of the workers class is called in every so often to attend a few meetings in order to applaud the speeches and to vote unanimously for the resolutions proposed. Basically, it is government by clique. A dictatorship certainly, but not a proletarian dictatorship. The dictatorship of a handful of politicians; dictatorship in the bourgeois meaning of the term, in the Jacobin meaning (postponing

the Congress of Soviets from three to six months!). Furthermore, such a situation inevitably leads to a complete degradation of public life: assassinations, shooting of hostages, etc.[28]

Rosa Luxemburg preferred not to make this piece of writing public because she believed that the Germans' mission was to act as a bridge between the Russian revolutionaries and the Social-Reformists of the West.[29] Such a bitter denunciation of Bolshevik methods would have prevented the German Left from carrying out any mediating role. She did, however, make clear to her close collaborators the extent of the divergence between herself and Lenin. For instance, when the Spartacus League became a political party in December 1918, she unsuccessfully suggested that they take on the name "socialist" rather than "communist."[30] In January 1919, her instructions to comrade Hugo Eberlein as he was leaving for Moscow were along similar lines. As Eberlein wrote a few years later, Luxemburg told him to oppose the idea of founding an international communist organization and to explain to the Bolsheviks that it was "premature."[31]

Meanwhile, between December 1918 and January 1919, revolutionary unrest grew within the Berlin labor movement. Many believed the time had come for insurrection. Hundreds of thousands of workers took to the streets and the atmosphere became heated and tense. Radek, who was in Berlin, had the task of applying the prudent directives Lenin had given him. He spoke out against insurrection and urged the workers to go back to their jobs. He recommended that any action the revolutionaries decided on be kept at the level of "protests." He proclaimed very clearly in print: "An attempt by the proletariat to seize power is unthinkable."[32]

Some among the Spartacists did not go along with such a cautious line. Karl Liebknecht, for one, became part of a revolutionary committee which announced that it was going to take the place of the Social Democratic government. Luxemburg took a different stance, though. Her prudent and realistic attitude seemed quite similar to Radek's, although she did not identify with his views. On the other hand, in the last article she wrote before her death, she defended the Berlin revolutionaries with arguments that revealed her determination to assure the primacy of Germany inside the international movement.[33] This primacy was short-lived, however, and a determining factor in its end was Luxemburg's death.

Rosa Luxemburg and Karl Liebknecht were forced to go into hiding on 12 January 1919. Three days later they were arrested, and the next day they were barbarously murdered by the soldiers who were holding them in custody. After their death Lenin's authority increased within the international revolutionary movement. As Pierre Broué has written, Luxemburg and Liebknecht "were the only ones among all the communists outside Russia who could debate on an equal basis with the Bolshevik leaders and could have acted as a counterweight to their authority in the new International."[34]

6
Russia's Difference

Lenin organized the Soviet state assuming world revolution was never going to take place. He asked the Soviets to mobilize for the long-term job of building the new-born state, counting only on themselves. He continually repeated that the era of agitation was over and that reconstruction had just begun. In March 1918 Lenin declared:

> The last war has been a bitter, painful, but serious lesson for the Russian people. It has taught them to organize, to become disciplined, to obey, to establish a discipline that will be exemplary. Learn discipline from Germans; for, if we do not, we, as a people, are doomed, we shall live in eternal slavery.[1]

Lenin had no hesitations about calling the Russian citizen "a bad worker" who was going to have to change, straighten up, and stop his laziness. Thanks to new rules and efficiency, the Soviet republic would be able to "cease being wretched and impotent and become mighty and abundant for all time."[2] On the subject of worker discipline, Lenin began expounding views in 1918 that would be incessantly repeated years later by Stalin's propaganda machine. Six months after Lenin took power, he was already stating that "heroism displayed in prolonged and persevering organizational work on a national scale is immensely more difficult than, but at the same time immensely superior to, heroism displayed in an uprising."[3]

He urged the Soviet press to muffle political debate, and to dedicate its efforts to propagandizing work and production:

> The Soviet press has devoted excessive space and attention to the petty political issues, the personal questions of political leadership by which the capitalists of all countries have striven to divert the attention of the masses from the really important, profound and fundamental questions of our life. . . . The problem is how to convert the press from an organ mainly devoted to communicating the political news of the day into a serious organ for educating the mass of the population in economics. We shall

have to ensure that the press serving the Soviet masses will devote less space to questions of the political composition of the political leadership, or to questions of the tenth-rate political measures that comprise the commonplace activity and the routine work of all political institutions. Instead the press will have to give priority to labor questions in their immediately practical setting.[4]

Lenin wanted there to be "ten times less," or better still "100 times less" newspaper material "devoted to the so-called current news." His aim was to have "distributed in hundreds of thousands and millions of copies, a press that acquaints the whole population with the exemplary arrangement of affairs in a few state labor communes which surpass the others."[5] The Bolshevik leader had as his objective a society that was depoliticized, disciplined, laborious, and obedient. He repeated insistently in September 1918:

Far too much space is being allotted to political agitation on outdated themes — to political ballyhoo — and far too little to the building of the new life, to the facts about it. . . .

Less politics. Politics has been "elucidated" fully and reduced to a struggle between the two camps: the insurrectionary proletariat and the handful of capitalist slaveowners (with the whole gang, right down to the Mensheviks and others). We must speak very briefly about these politics.

More economics. But not in the sense of "general" discussions, learned reviews, intellectual plans and similar piffle, for, I regret to say, they are all too often just piffle and nothing more. By economics we mean the gathering, *careful checking* and study of the facts of the actual organization of the new life. Have *real* successes been achieved by big factories, agricultural communes, the Poor Peasants' Committees, and local Economic Councils in building up the new economy?[6]

The grave economic crisis that struck Russia, the desertion of cities, the misery and famine that hit Moscow and Petrograd — all this led Lenin to give primary importance to the resumption of production. To that end, he was ready to introduce piece-work pay and even capitalistic methods of work organization such as the Taylor system.[7] Along with these remedies, he trusted in the courts:

Dictatorship, however, presupposes a revolutionary government that is really firm and ruthless in crushing both exploiters and hooligans, and our government is too mild. Obedience, and unquestioning obedience at that, during work to the one-man decisions of Soviet directors, of the dictators elected or appointed by Soviet institutions, vested with dictatorial powers (as is demanded, for example, by the railway decree), is far, very far from being guaranteed as yet.[8]

For the Russian workers, the revolution was a rebellion against the past, the advent of a new world in which they, not someone else, would control the factories. Lenin was forced to disappoint them. Faced with the total disorganization that had rapidly spread through production processes, he decided to bury "workers' control" forever.[9] In January 1918, he announced that in the factories "the strict regularity of a machine enterprise" had to replace "the mixed form of discussions and meetings."[10] The leader of the Bolsheviks intended to react against the anarchy, lack of realism, and absence of discipline of revolutionaries and of Russians in general. "It has to be learnt," continued Lenin, "that it is impossible to live in modern society without machines, without discipline — one has either to master modern techniques or be crushed."[11]

On the eve of the revolution, in the pages of *The State and Revolution*, Lenin had claimed that public administration was going to be very easy, within the reach of anyone who could read, write, and do arithmetic.[12] But in 1918, he came to exactly the opposite conclusion. He denied that running the government was an easy thing, confessing that the Bolsheviks were in an especially inferior condition where practical activities were concerned: "We are not often short of propagandists, but our most crying shortage is the lack of efficient leaders and organizers."[13] Lenin expressed similar thoughts even more openly in March 1919, when he admitted: "The Soviet apparatus is accessible to all the working people in word, but actually it is far from being accessible to all of them, as we all know."[14]

Two years later, he criticized the proletariat's lack of political abilities: "Does every worker know how to run the state? People working in a practical sphere know that this is not true."[15] Lenin certainly belonged to the category of practical people. He was convinced that in order to build a modern state, the Bolsheviks had to learn from the bourgeoisie, make use of bourgeois experts, and try to construct together with them a system of production such as already existed in Germany and England.[16] Russia was not ready for socialism and Lenin knew that perfectly well. He realized fully how strange it was that the Bolsheviks had succeeded in taking over in such a relatively backward country. In order to protect their tenuous hold on power, he was ready to resort to compromise and use all the weapons available, including state terror.

In the early days of Lenin's government, he hesitated to use institutionalized terror: "We have not resorted, and I hope will not resort, to the

terrorism of the French revolutionaries who guillotined unarmed men," he announced on 17 November 1917.[17] He knew the use of terror would be in sharp contrast to the democratic and humanitarian approach of the West's socialist parties.[18] Not even a month had passed, though, before Lenin started to behave just like the French revolutionaries. On 11 December, he proclaimed that the Constitutional-Democrats, the so-called "Cadets," were "enemies of the people" and that all their leaders were liable to arrest. He declared: "We are not merely persecuting non-observers of formalities, we are levelling direct political accusations against a political party."[19]

From the beginning of 1918 onward, he encouraged his followers to carry out executions without trial. In January, he wrote that in order to rid Russia of the rich, the scoundrels, and the parasites (workers included), various means were to be used:

> In one place half a score of rich, a dozen rogues, half a dozen workers who shirk their work (in the manner of rowdies, the manner in which many compositors in Petrograd, particularly in the party printing-shops, shirk their work) will be put in prison. In another place they will be put to cleaning latrines. In a third place they will be provided with "yellow tickets" after they have served their time, so that everyone shall keep an eye on them, as *harmful* persons, until they reform. In a fourth place, one out of every ten idlers will be shot on the spot.[20]

At the beginning of 1918, the All-Russia Conference of Commissars of Justice was held in Moscow. Some of the delegates, who were all either Bolsheviks or pro-Bolsheviks, protested because the secret police (the Cheka) that Lenin had set up were in action in the provinces, shooting, arresting, and committing abuses of all kinds, without anyone exerting any kind of control over them. They were already behaving like "a state within a state."[21] A virtual reign of terror began in July, when a plot by the Left Socialist Revolutionaries failed. The terror spread in August after Fanja Kaplan shot Lenin. On 31 August, Stalin telegraphed that the Bolsheviks of Tsaritsyn (the future Stalingrad), by way of reprisal, had instituted "open and systematic mass terrorism against the bourgeoisie and its agents."[22] Mass executions took place all over Bolshevik Russia; more than 500 people were put to death in Petrograd alone.[23]

These events help clarify not only Lenin's domestic policy but also his foreign policy, and they demonstrate what kind of unscrupulous "realism" he resorted to. They also indicate to what extent he departed from his ideals, and how many compromises and about-faces he was prepared to make. Hence, they show how different Russian Bolshevism was from most European socialist movements. It is not surprising, then, that Lenin tried to open up his country to the outside world not in the direction of those who would call for respect for principles and ideals, but rather toward those states which demanded above all respect for the rules and for "reasons of state."

7
Lenin Seeks an Accord with the Victors

The defeat of Germany in the autumn of 1918 convinced Lenin to look to the Entente powers for his guarantee of survival, since it was the Allies who seemed to hold the fate of the world in their hands. As long as the war lasted, many Bolsheviks felt that the Soviet state could save its revolutionary principles and also obtain some concrete results, if it limited its actions to "maneuvering" between Germany and the Allies. Upon Germany's defeat, this possibility seemed to disappear. In answer to Lev Kamenev, who apparently had some misgivings about Soviet foreign policies, Lenin wrote in October 1918:

> About "the fine theory of manoeuvring." All theories are good *if* they correspond to objective reality. But our reality has changed, for if Germany is defeated, it becomes impossible to manoeuvre, for there are no longer the two belligerents, *between whom we were manoeuvring*!
> *Attention.* Britain would gobble us up, were it not for . . . the Red Army.[1]

Lenin was counting solely on the Red Army. He made no reference to any help that might come from the spread of revolution in Europe. During those very days, indeed, he discounted such an eventuality on the pages of *Pravda*:

> Europe's greatest misfortune and danger is that it has no revolutionary party. It has parties of traitors like the Scheidemanns, Renaudels, Hendersons, Webbs and Co., and servile souls like Kautsky. But it has no revolutionary party.[2]

Consequently, from October 1918 onwards, Lenin attempted to establish contacts with the Allies in order to reach an accord and obtain diplomatic recognition. On 11 October, Chicherin sent Ioffe a message that indicated to what point the Soviets were ready to accept conditions laid down by the victors:

> At any time, we . . . are prepared to do what is necessary to secure peace for us, if only the conditions will be acceptable. This task is one of the most important for all our representatives who have the possibility of meeting with representatives of the Entente or politicians connected with them. While not appearing too eager and not conveying the impression that it seems we are crying for mercy, it is necessary, if the opportunity offers itself, to make it understood that we desire nothing but to live in peace with everyone. They must tell us their conditions. Of course, we are unable to sanction an occupation by the Entente replacing that of the Germans. If they will tell us precisely what they want, however, we will consider it.[3]

Soviet Russia was prepared to make concessions to the Entente countries that were even greater than those they had made to Germany. After all, now that the Entente had been victorious in the First World War, it might be tempted to solve the Bolshevik problem through force. Lenin's behavior throughout the year 1919 demonstrated that he was as distraught as he had been at the time of Brest-Litovsk, if not more so.

There can be no mistake about how to interpret the note Chicherin sent to the President of the United States, Woodrow Wilson, on 24 October 1918. The American President, who had promised in his "Fourteen Points" international cooperation and the evacuation of foreign troops from all Russian territories, had then proceeded to act in a way that did not conform to these promises. Lenin saw an opportunity to turn these broken promises to Soviet advantage. He ordered Chicherin to send Wilson a diplomatic note that was "very detailed, courteous, but venomous." As for its substance, he wanted to make it known that the Bolsheviks were prepared to offer important concessions. They were even ready to discuss once again the debt of 17 billion rubles contracted by the czarist regime with capitalist countries — a debt that the Soviet Central Executive Committee had cancelled in February:

> Do the capitalists want some of the forests in the north, part of Siberia, interest on 17 thousand millions? If so, then surely they won't make a secret of it. We propose to you: state outright, *how much*?[4]

The long document composed by Chicherin departed from the norms of diplomatic style. As Louis Fischer has remarked: "This unusual note was a combination of pure revolutionary propaganda and shrewd diplomacy. The Bolsheviks hoped that their offer to pay old debts would pave the way to negotiations and to a cessation of armed foreign intervention."[5]

President Wilson did not reply to the note, but the Soviet leaders persisted. On 3 November, Chicherin sent for the ranking diplomatic representative from Sweden and asked him to inform Great Britain that the Soviets were ready to sign an armistice with the British and the other Entente powers. During the same month, the Congress of Soviets issued a proclamation that called for the opening of peace negotiations. Meanwhile, between November and December, Allied forces landed in Odessa and the Caucasus. On 2 December, Chicherin formally protested to the Allies over the landing, but he also reaffirmed his country's readiness to come to an agreement and he repeated that Russia "only demanded to be left in peace." In Stockholm, on 23 December, Soviet representative Maksim Litvinov communicated once more to the Allies that his government desired to settle all pending questions with them.[6] The following day, Litvinov telegraphed a respectfully worded message to President Wilson, saying that he had been authorized to open negotiations on behalf of Soviet Russia. He concluded with the words, "I venture to appeal to your sense of justice and impartiality. I hope and trust, above all, that before deciding on any course of action you will give justice to the demand of *audiatur et altera pars*."[7]

Then, on 25 December, Litvinov, together with V.C. Vorovsky, visited the leader of Norway's Social Democrats, Ludwig Meyer. The Soviet representative enumerated the concessions that Russia was ready to offer the Allies: a political amnesty, a removal of press censorship, self-determination for Poland, the Ukraine, etc., and a re-examination of the czarist regime's foreign debt. Lenin's government, furthermore, was prepared to "desist from carrying on any propaganda in the Allied countries which could be construed as interference with their internal affairs." The Soviets had essentially two requests in return: economic and technical aid for reconstruction and an end to Allied military operations, including any type of help to the White forces.[8] On his part, Chicherin sent a note to the government in Washington on 12 January 1919, in which he summarized all the recent steps that Moscow had taken to bring about peace, and he ended with the words, "It lies therefore with you, not with us, if such a settlement has not yet been arranged."[9]

At about the same time, the advocates of an agreement with the Soviets became active in the capitals of the Allied countries. In London, Prime Minister David Lloyd George was one of the principal supporters of an accord with Lenin. During a meeting of the War Cabinet on 31 December, Lloyd George announced his opposition to military expeditions against the Bolsheviks. He pointed out that there were not enough troops to wage war in Russia. Besides, anti-Soviet military intervention would be counterproductive since it would bring greater unity to Lenin's state and contribute to the spreading of Bolshevism to England itself. The only thing left to do was to invite all the Russians — Bolsheviks and anti-Bolsheviks — to declare a truce and send delegations to a peace conference.[10]

The Americans, too, gave signs of being favorable to negotiations with Moscow. They took concrete action in that direction, sending a diplomat to Stockholm in order to meet with Litvinov. The U.S. representative was William H. Buckler, an attaché at the London Embassy and half-brother of Henry White, ex-Ambassador to Rome and Paris. Buckler met with Litvinov on 14, 15, and 16 January 1919, and sent his superiors a detailed report on the meetings. "The Soviet government's conciliatory attitude is unquestionable," he reported. He confirmed that the Soviets were ready to renegotiate the czarist debt and to cease Bolshevik propaganda abroad "at once if peace were made." He remarked that the Soviets gave scant credibility to revolution in the West: "It is realized by Russians that conditions are not favorable for a revolution of the Russian type in certain Western countries. No amount of propaganda could produce such a result." Naturally, Buckler did not neglect to mention that "a large part of the Bolsheviks" opposed Chicherin's and Litvinov's plans for compromise."[11]

The Allies had two choices. They could either take Lenin and Chicherin at their word and open negotiations to reach a suitable compromise with them, or they could go to war with Russia, bring down the Bolsheviks, and support other political forces with whom, then, agreement could be reached. The Allies were not able to come to any decision, however. They lacked resoluteness and appeared undecided, uneasy, and in disarray. Their policy toward Russia was a failure. What the Allies most feared was a war with the Soviets. Although their forces had landed at Murmansk, Archangel, Vladivostok, Odessa, and the Caucasus the year before, a real war was still not being waged. At the end of the year, after having defeated Germany and Austria, the Allies could have used their armies to defeat Bolshevism. But in January 1919, during the meetings held in Paris, the Allied leaders judged it unwise to commit themselves to such an undertaking. Lloyd George repeated what he had declared a few days earlier to his fellow cabinet members. He asserted that war in Russia was not feasible since it required too many men and means. He reminded his colleagues that in 1918, when Bolshevism was militarily weaker, the Germans had had to deploy one million men to occupy only a few of the provinces of Russia's former empire. How many men would be needed to occupy the whole country now that Bolshevism was more solidly entrenched and better armed? Lloyd George added that if British troops received the order to go and fight in Russia, they would rebel. President Wilson, French Premier Clemenceau, and Italian Prime Minister Orlando agreed on the impossibility of war. Wilson, a professed anti-czarist,

Lenin Seeks an Accord with the Victors

stated specifically that, "British and American troops were unwilling to fight in Russia because they feared their efforts might lead to the restoration of the old order, which was even more disastrous than the present one." He explained that Bolshevism had sympathizers even among the American rich.[12] Within the individual Allied governments there were, of course, supporters of massive military intervention against the Bolsheviks — among them was Winston Churchill — but these interventionists did not carry the day.[13]

8

Bullitt's Mission

The Allies met in Paris to define the new world order. But could it be determined without Bolshevik Russia? Many delegates from the Allied countries wanted to invite representatives of Lenin's government to Paris. Others, especially the French, did not, so a compromise was agreed upon. The Allies decided, first of all, that not only should the Bolsheviks be invited, but also "every organized group that exercises or tries to exercise authority" within the borders of Russia's ex-empire. Hence, they convoked the anti-Soviet organizations of the Whites' generals. They also announced that, as a preliminary move, all these groups would have to declare a truce.

Secondly, the Allies decided the Soviets ought not to be admitted to the conference in Paris itself. A neutral site was chosen, in a kind of diplomatic "quarantine" — the small Turkish island of Prinkipo, opposite Constantinople. It was a location the Soviets could reach by sea without having to cross through territory of any of the Allied powers. Lastly, they arranged the meeting in such a way that it did not imply diplomatic recognition of Soviet Russia. The Soviet representatives were being invited solely to discuss how to bring order and peace to their country.

The Prinkipo meeting was to take place on 15 February and President Wilson composed a message inviting the Russians.[1] This telegraphed message was never received by the Soviet government, probably because the French, who were against the whole idea, stopped it at the Paris telegraph office.[2] On 23 January, however, the Soviets received indirect news of the planned encounter and wired President Wilson for confirmation. After receiving no reply, they proceeded to wire the Paris socialist newspaper, *Le Populaire*, and this time they received a confirmation.[3]

It is evident that the Soviets received an invitation that was as insufficient in form as it was deficient in content. Nonetheless, they accepted immediately and enthusiastically, according to the accounts given a few weeks later to American journalist Frazier Hunt by eyewitnesses:

I was told the Soviet leaders welcomed the invitation to the Prinkipo conference. Men whom the world considered cruel, blood-thirsty and mad hugged each other, crying with joy, when they heard the news that they would be able to speak freely to the world and to their opponents.[4]

In a wire to Trotsky, Lenin wrote: "I think you will have to go to Wilson." The head of the Bolsheviks was afraid, however, that Wilson wanted "to secure for himself Siberia and part of the south."[5]

On 4 February Chicherin informed the Allies that his government was willing to accept annexation by the Allied powers of territory belonging to Russia's ex-empire. The Soviets were also prepared to recognize the czarist debts, pay interest in the form of raw materials on newly acquired debts, guarantee mineral rights and forest products to foreign capitalists, and restrain their propaganda in the Entente countries. Lenin's government was even ready to discuss Soviet Russia's internal situation with the Allies, since this situation "will necessarily affect the extent of the proposed concessions."[6]

After reading Chicherin's note, the revolutionary parties of Europe were stunned. For the first time they realized what direction Soviet foreign policy was moving in. The Brest-Litovsk peace treaty had already caused dismay, although it was generally considered an act of dire necessity following the advance of the German troops. But this time? In a newspaper of the Italian socialists, *Avanti!*, an editorial signed with the initials A.G., probably for Antonio Gramsci, flatly stated that Lenin's Russia was beginning to accept the capitalist world: "This is the painful meaning that emerges from the diplomatic note comrade Chicherin sent to the governments of the Entente."[7] However, the promptness with which the Bolsheviks accepted the Prinkipo conference invitation did them little good. While the Entente countries were naming their delegates to the meeting, the anti-Bolshevik groups announced their refusal to sit at the same table with Trotsky. As a result, the plans fell through.[8]

While Moscow was impatient to reach an agreement, many Westerners were equally anxious to open discussions with the Soviets. They knew that peace in Europe and the world would not be complete if Russia were ignored. On 18 February 1919, U.S. Secretary of State Robert Lansing secretly designated one of his aides, William Bullitt, to leave Paris for Moscow to meet with Lenin. Lloyd George was informed of the delicate mission entrusted to the American emissary. Bullitt, a young diplomat, belonged to the "liberal" aristocracy that felt some sympathy for the Soviet experiment. Indeed, several years later, William Bullitt was to marry Louise Bryant, the widow of John Reed.[9]

Bullitt's Mission

The American envoy arrived in Russia on 8 March, and in the following days met with Lenin, Chicherin, and Litvinov. On 14 March, Chicherin delivered the Soviet peace proposals to Bullitt. They were even more favorable to the Entente than those previously presented. The Soviet government reconfirmed the concessions already offered, adding that all the de facto governments existing in the ex-Russian empire could remain in possession of the territories they already controlled. It has been calculated that Lenin was giving up an immense amount of territory, corresponding to four-fifths of today's Soviet Union.[10] At that time, non-Bolshevik governments were in control of the Baltic, the White Sea, part of White Russia, half of the Ukraine, the Crimea, the Caucasus, the region of the Urals, and all of Siberia. Perhaps Lenin hoped to recover those territories in the future, but for the time being, he accepted the idea of leaving them in the hands of Denikin, Kolchak, and his other enemies. One cannot help wondering what the course of world history would have been if these extraordinary concessions of Lenin's had led to an accord.

Bullitt wired Lenin's proposals to President Wilson. He specified that the Soviet leaders had expressed to him "in the most straightforward, unequivocal manner" their determination to pay the foreign debts. He ended his message with the following words: "There is no doubt whatever of the desire of the Soviet government for a just and reasonable peace, or of the sincerity of this proposal, and I pray you will consider it with the deepest seriousness."[11]

In a memorandum dated the end of March, Bullitt noted that though Trotsky and other Bolsheviks still wanted to promote revolution in France and England, Lenin, Chicherin, and the majority of the party did not. They were convinced that, for the moment, the fundamental problem was saving the proletariat of Russia and Europe from hunger. Lenin had previously declared that a European revolution would accomplish little if as a result the U.S. government made Europe go hungry. According to Bullitt, therefore, Lenin and Chicherin "advocate the conciliation of the United States even at the cost of compromising with many of the principles they hold most dear."[12]

In 1919, as in 1918, many Bolsheviks disagreed with Lenin's unprincipled pragmatism. One of them, Cristian Rakovsky, head of the Ukrainian soviets and one of Trotsky's followers, spoke out publicly against an agreement with the Allies.[13] During Bullitt's stay in Moscow, Chicherin wrote Cristian Rakovsky in an attempt to change his mind. "The decision is very important," he explained, referring to the determination to negotiate with Bullitt: "If we don't try to get an agreement, the policy of blockade will be pressed with vigor. They will send tanks ... to Denikin, Kolchak, Petliura, Paderewski." According to Chicherin, Bullitt did not believe that the Bolsheviks could obtain much in the way of concessions from the Allies, but he still hoped to carry out his mission successfully. "France knows nothing about it. This must be kept absolutely secret," he admonished in his note to Rakovsky.[14] At the same time, Lenin tried to prepare the Bolshevik party for the costly agreement with the Allies. He explained that the Entente countries were extremely powerful and repeatedly referred to the experience of the Brest-Litovsk peace treaty.[15]

Bullitt returned to Paris on 15 March, and was welcomed enthusiastically by President Wilson's closest aide, Colonel House, but was not received by Wilson himself. He met with Lloyd George, who was favorably inclined toward an agreement with Lenin, though he admitted to Bullitt, waving a copy of the *Daily Mail* at him, that he feared the reaction of British public opinion. Journalist Henry Wickham Steed, editor of both the *Daily Mail* and the *Times*, has recounted in his memoirs how much he did to bury Bullitt's mission and to prevent Lloyd George and the Allies from furnishing credentials, directly or indirectly, to that evil thing that was Bolshevism.[16]

One of the reasons that convinced the Allies not to accept Lenin's offers was that the White armies seemed about to destroy Bolshevism in the spring of 1919. During the past year the Red Army had lost Kharkov, Orel, Samara, and Kazan, and was now reduced to a territory which was not much larger than the principality of Moscovia. Hence, the Allies felt free to refuse even the most advantageous offers, under the misconception that Soviet Russia was on the verge of collapse. Although the Allies missed the historic opportunity that Bullitt's mission offered them, Lenin persevered in his efforts for several months. In an interview to French journalist Ludovic Nadeau, he declared that the communist state could get along with capitalist states, and he added that he was willing "not with pleasure, it is true, but with resignation" to cede territories of Russia's ex-empire.[17]

On 6 May 1919, Lenin sent a letter to Chicherin and Litvinov instructing them on how to answer Norwegian representative F. Nansen, who had presented himself in the role of mediator between Soviet Russia and the Allies. The reply was to be negative, said the instructions, if the offer were for a mere "truce"; affirmative if it were for a real "peace." In the same note, he expressed his discontent over the failure of Bullitt's mission.[18] Then, in June, after having held off for months, Lenin authorized Litvinov to make public the proposition made to Bullitt. Litvinov delivered a copy to American foreign correspondent Isaac Don Levine in Moscow, who printed it in the New York *Globe*, on 5 June, creating considerable sensation and surprise.[19] A month later, replying to questions asked by the United Press news agency, Lenin confirmed that the proposals he had made to Bullitt were still good:

We have, on many occasions, given a precise, clear and written exposition of the terms upon which we agree to conclude peace with Kolchak, Denikin and Mannerheim — for instance to Bullitt who conducted negotiations with us (and with me personally in Moscow) on behalf of the United States Government, in a letter to Nansen, etc. It is not our fault that the governments of the United States and other countries are afraid to publish those documents in full and that they hide the truth from the people. I will mention only our basic condition: we are prepared to pay all debts to France and other countries provided there is a real peace and not peace in words alone, i.e., if it is formally signed and ratified by the governments of Great Britain, France, the United States, Japan and Italy.[20]

Once again, in October 1919, in answer to queries from a *Chicago Daily News* correspondent, Lenin repeated in vain:

Our policy is the former, that is, we have accepted the peace propositions of Mr. Bullitt. We have never changed our peace conditions formulated with Mr. Bullitt.... We are decidedly for an economic understanding with America — with all countries but *especially* with America. If necessary we can give you the full text of our peace conditions as formulated by our government with Mr. Bullitt.[21]

That same month, Chicherin received a visit from a liberal member of the British Parliament, Colonel Cecil B. Malone, to whom he handed peace proposals which were quite similar to those previously given to Bullitt. Colonel Malone reported on the visit to the House of Commons on 5 November 1919.[22]

Meanwhile, the Bolsheviks were going through a very crucial phase of the civil war. In autumn 1919, the military situation took such a turn for the worse that Lenin began making preparations to go back underground. For this purpose, the Bolsheviks were arranging for large sums of money and a good number of counterfeit passports.[23] But in general the Russians were tired of wars and revolutions. The common man was not at all involved in world revolution. As Levine put it in one of his reports from Moscow, "the people desire only to let the rest of the world alone, provided they are let alone. They are fighting for peace in Russia and not for social revolution in Western Europe."[24]

9

The Founding of the Comintern

The international communist organization, the Comintern, was founded in Moscow on 4 March 1919 through Lenin's initiative. It was inaugurated on the eve of Bullitt's arrival in Russia. Indeed, he was present at the huge demonstration that took place in Petrograd to mark the occasion.[1]

The creation of the Comintern was very much in line with the foreign policy objectives that Lenin was pursuing at the time. It was surely no coincidence that, together with Lenin, Foreign Commissar Chicherin coordinated and directed the whole constituent assembly. Besides being one of the delegates, Chicherin was also co-author of the letter of invitation to the assembly and chairman of the commission that verified the delegates' authority. After this inaugural congress was over, he kept the Comintern under direct control by placing one of his closest aides, Vorovsky, in the secretariat. In brief, the Comintern's constituent assembly was organized and directed by the upper echelons of Soviet Russia.

There were thirty-four delegates, supposedly representing twenty-four different parties from as many countries. However, thirty of them were communists residing in Russia but originally from other countries, who had no mandate from the parties of these countries. Almost all of them were members of one sole party — the Russian Communist party.[2] Two of the four delegates who were not residents of Russia, a Norwegian and a Swede, represented countries without communist parties. The third non-resident delegate, Eberlein from Germany, was against the foundation of the Comintern. The fourth, the Austrian Karl Steinhardt, was really the only delegate who had the proper qualifications — he did not live in Russia, he represented a non-Russian communist movement, albeit a small one, and he backed the plan of establishing the Comintern. Thanks to the presence of the almost unknown Steinhardt, Lenin obtained approval of the constitution of the new International.[3]

As mentioned earlier, German delegate Hugo Eberlein had received instructions from Rosa Luxemburg to oppose the creation of a communist International.[4] It would be "premature," in Luxemburg's opinion, and should not take place until communist parties came into being in the major European countries. After the death of Luxemburg and Liebknecht, the German communist leaders told Eberlein to continue opposing the plan. As soon as the delegate from Germany arrived in Moscow, he explained his mandate to Lenin, who told Eberlein he was not surprised.[5]

The thirty-four delegates who participated in the First Congress of the Comintern held meetings in the Kremlin from 2 to 6 March 1919. Eberlein's persistent opposition placed the Bolshevik delegation in such a difficult position, however, that at one point Zinoviev felt forced to request that the Comintern's founding be postponed. Then, as Angelica Balabanova has recounted in her memoirs, something happened that changed the whole atmosphere of the meeting:

> The meeting was on the point of being adjourned without having accomplished a great deal when something occurred that, for us all, except probably the members of the Russian Communist Party, was totally unexpected, and it changed the whole situation. A typographer of Austrian origin [Karl Steinhardt], who had been taken prisoner by the Russians and subsequently had become an ardent Bolshevik, after having sneaked back into Western Europe, returned to Moscow at the very moment the meeting was breaking up. Clearly showing signs of a hard trip back, he excitedly gave a detailed and enthusiastic account of his journey. All of Western Europe, he said, beginning with Germany and Austria, was on the eve of a triumphant social revolution. "All eyes are turned towards revolutionary Russia," he went on. "They are only waiting for her to give them the password to go into action." (Shortly after that, Steinhardt was one of the first Western workers to break away from the communist movement.)
>
> This fiery speech, partly spontaneous and sincere, and partly suggested by Radek, was made to remove all doubts from those who considered the creation of a new International not only premature but illegal. With well-timed tactics, one of the "delegates" asked for another round of votes. This time, everybody, except the German delegate, decided that the meeting should be considered the First Congress of the Third International.[6]

Hugo Eberlein, the only delegate who represented a communist party of a certain size, still did not want to vote in favor, and abstained. Hence, the Third International came into being artificially, over German opposition, and without a group of communist parties in Europe that it could count on.

Lenin wanted the new organism for the following reasons. First of all, now that the war was over, the Second International of social democratic parties was being reconstituted. A conference had been held in Bern from 3 to 10 February 1919. Lenin had to take some prestige away from the Social Democrats and demonstrate that communist internationalism was able to found its own organization. If he did not, the communist movement would look to the world as if it were disintegrating. The motion passed on 4 March that instituted the Comintern included the admission: "If the conference convoked in Moscow were not to create the Third International, it might give the impression that the communist parties were in disagreement among themselves. This would bring discredit upon our position and increase the confusion among those elements of the proletariat that are vacillating in all countries."[7]

Lenin's second reason was to exploit a myth of Bolshevism that had spread worldwide among socialist organizations, according to which Soviet Russia seemed to realize their aspirations. Lenin was desperately searching for outside support and he could not waste the opportunities that this myth offered him. He hoped to set up a centralized network of communist parties capable of "subordinating the interest of the movement within each country to the common interests of the revolution on an international scale," as he wrote in the letter of invitation that had been sent to the communists of the world.[8] The other parties of the Comintern would be subordinated to Russia's, as Lenin explicitly put it: "Leadership in the revolutionary proletarian International has passed for a time — for a short time, it goes without saying — to the Russians, just as at various periods of the nineteenth century it was in the hands of the British, then of the French, then of the Germans."[9]

Lenin's third reason for setting up the Comintern involved domestic concerns, since many Bolsheviks did not agree at all with their leader's "nationalist" tendencies. They were still planning revolution on a global scale, which they saw as the key to enabling Russia to overcome her political isolation and make an economic comeback. The existence of the Comintern would give these Bolsheviks the feeling that something was moving in the right direction.

Finally, Lenin saw that the Comintern would serve him very well in pursuing his objectives in foreign politics. The policy of coexistence with the West did not imply any kind of immediate "ideological disarmament." In various messages sent to the Allies, Chicherin and Litvinov promised to stop revolutionary propaganda only after a peace settlement had been signed. Until peace was concluded, the fact that the Third International existed, even if only on paper, strengthened the Bolsheviks' diplomatic position.

Later, subordination of the national movements to the "common interests of international revolution" would permit Russia to direct the parties of the Comintern, according to the exigencies of "reasons of state."

Founded on such a precarious base, the Comintern remained an inefficient organization for some time. Angelica Balabanova, who became its secretary in 1919, has written in her memoirs that it was simply a "bureaucratic institution."[10] In recent times, communist historian Aldo Agosti has acknowledged that in 1919 "the ability of the Comintern to have an effective impact on the course of events was practically nil."[11] Lenin was not able to establish ties with the socialist and communist movements of Western Europe. The appeals that Moscow sent out took months to arrive at their destinations. According to Aldo Agosti, for all of the year 1919, the Comintern was "not at all that 'world party of revolution' that it aspired to be." It was only "the small nucleus of an organization which was, for the most part, still to be created." Its organizational weakness persisted during the following year, as the communist historian has confirmed: "Until well into 1920, the situation was such that the major European Communist parties found it impossible to send their representatives to the Communist International's Executive Committee."[12]

The Comintern, then, did not really begin to function until the late summer of 1920, when the Bolshevik government was enacting its New Economic Policy (NEP) and was no longer talking of world revolution, not even as sheer propaganda. In effect, Lenin never considered the Comintern a suitable means for initiating such a revolution.

10

The Revolution in Hungary

Several revolutionary uprisings took place in Europe between the end of 1918 and 1919, but they proved to be fleeting experiments in communist power. The one that lasted the longest occurred in Hungary, where the communists remained in power for 133 days. Even Hungary's experience, however, serves to demonstrate that Lenin did not put his trust in the spread of revolution through Europe.

The Hungarian Republic of Soviets came into being on 21 March 1919, a few days after the founding of the Comintern.[1] Immediately after, several Social Democrat leaders of the new government began expressing their hopes that their country would not become overly tied to Soviet Russia and would come to some kind of agreement with the West.[2] Bela Kun, leader of the Hungarian communists, who officially held the post of Commissar for Foreign Affairs but for all practical purposes was the new head of state, sent a message to the governments of the Entente powers. He declared that Hungary wanted to live in peace with everyone and that the alliance with Russia which the new regime had announced, far from being a declaration of war, did not even signify a break with the Entente.[3]

The Entente governments, meeting in Paris at the time, decided to send an envoy to Hungary. The choice fell on General Jan Smuts, Prime Minister of South Africa and member of the British empire's War Cabinet. On 1 April, Smuts left on a mission whose purpose, according to the testimony of some, was not only to seek a solution to the Hungarian question, but also to find out if Bela Kun was in a position to act as intermediary between the Entente and Lenin.[4] Two days before his departure, General Smuts was present at the meeting that Bullitt, who was just back from Russia, had with Lloyd George. The South African had read Bullitt's memorandum on the possibilities of coming to agreement with Lenin, and had found it worth consideration.[5] Now it was the General's turn to leave for Budapest and perhaps Moscow. On the day he left, Smuts confided to a friend that he hoped the objective of his mission went beyond Hungary, and in that case he would be gone longer than expected.[6]

As it turned out, General Smuts did not go on to Moscow, and he remained in Budapest only two days. He and Bela Kun discussed the territorial disputes that Hungary was having with Romania. He asked Kun to pull his troops back to the line of demarcation that the Allied powers had fixed and he offered Hungary a few territorial concessions in return. Fearing the reaction of public opinion and the army, Kun procrastinated, and Smuts left Hungary without getting Kun to sign an accord. Before leaving Budapest, he wired his impressions to Paris. He was convinced that there was no hostility toward the great powers on Hungary's part. The communist government was weak and sharply divided, however. This made it likely that it would fall before too long.[7]

The new Hungarian government was, indeed, very weak. On 2 April, it acknowledged that recruitment of volunteers for the "Red Army" was turning into a failure; the only trustworthy unit was the "international regiment."[8] The Paris daily *Le Temps* reported that, according to General Smuts, the authority of the communists did not extend beyond the suburbs of Budapest.[9] A few months later, an eminent Hungarian communist, Eugene Varga, admitted that most of the proletariat did not support Bela Kun's government.[10]

Kun, with his fragile hold on power, failed to reach an accord with the Allies for reasons of domestic politics, not because Moscow persuaded him not to negotiate. During that time, Moscow was eager to negotiate with the West, and on 18 June 1919, Lenin wrote to Kun specifically to encourage him to open negotiations with the Allies: "They should be begun and carried on; it is necessary to make the fullest possible use of every opportunity to obtain a temporary armistice or peace, in order to give the people a breathing space."[11]

Most probably, Lenin was worried that the existence of the new Hungarian regime might cause him useless complications in pursuing Russian foreign policy. In the West, public opinion did not differentiate between Lenin's Russia and Kun's Hungary, and one might be held co-responsible for whatever the other did. But, in reality, the Budapest revolution was quite autonomous. Hungary's republic of soviets had come about and was held in place thanks to an alliance of the communists and the Social Democrats. This did not go down well in Moscow. As early as 23 March, Lenin had wired Bela Kun a communiqué reading: "Please inform us what real guarantees you have that the new Hungarian Government will actually be a communist, and not simply a socialist government, i.e., one of traitor-socialists."[12]

To complicate matters further, Kun was very actively engaged in initiatives involving countries bordering on Hungary. He was doing this totally on his own, and one can only imagine what Lenin's worried reactions must have been. During the brief period in which he held power, Bela Kun managed to send emissaries, money, and directives to the revolutionary movements in Austria, Yugoslavia, and Czechoslovakia, and his aims included promoting revolution throughout Europe. In June 1919, the army of the new Hungarian government invaded Slovakia and set up a republic of soviets. The following month the Hungarian troops withdrew from Slovakia and the republic of soviets collapsed (its communist leaders fleeing to Hungary). During those same weeks, several Yugoslavian communist leaders, financed by Kun, plotted insurrection in their country and were promptly arrested.[13] Two months earlier, the head of Hungary's communists had sent an envoy to Austria in the person of Ernoe Bettelheim, a Budapest lawyer and member of the Hungarian Communist party's Central Committee. In June, Bettelheim, along with some Austrian communist leaders, organized a daring if short-lived insurrection in Vienna which came to an end with a toll of twenty dead, several wounded, and about a hundred communists arrested.[14]

Bela Kun's revolutionary foreign politics amounted to a series of failures and disasters which risked compromising all the patient diplomacy the Bolshevik government had being carrying on. It is not clear what Lenin thought of Kun back in 1919, but he held the Hungarian in very low esteem by the year 1921. Among the delegates to the Third Congress of the Comintern that year was Italian author and communist Ignazio Silone, who reported that he was dumbstruck to hear Lenin say "When I hear some piece of foolishness going around my first reaction is to think that it must come from Bela Kun."[15] Moreover, during the Second Congress of the Comintern in 1920, though many issues were discussed, Hungary's revolutionary experiment was practically never mentioned.[16]

It is often said that Lenin did all he could to tie himself militarily to Kun's Hungary by moving the Red Army toward the West. The hypothesis is even advanced that the only reason both armies never united was because of the critical situation the Red Army was facing during the spring and summer of 1919. Two of Lenin's messages, however, lead one to doubt this version of events.

In April, the commander in chief of the Red Army, Joakim G. Vatsetis, asked Lenin's opinion about whether it was "politically opportune" to advance into Galizia and Bukovina in order to link up with the Hungarians. It is very likely that not only the communists in Budapest, but also many communists in Moscow were pressuring Vatsetis for this revolutionary liaison. Lenin sent his answer to the commander in chief on 21 or 22 April 1919, declaring he was not opposed to the idea of linking up — on the contrary, he considered it necessary. But, this having been said, he went on to state his reserves. The impression he wanted to leave was evidently that he deemed a link-up to be of secondary importance. And, in effect, it never came to pass.[17]

Three months later, Bela Kun wrote Lenin to protest over the lack of assistance and to call Chicherin and Ukrainian leader Rakovsky to account. In his reply, Lenin told Kun, "Do not worry too much." Then he announced in a biting tone that the accusations and suspicions directed at his collaborators had "absolutely no foundation whatever." He asserted that he himself was co-responsible for what was done or not done in regard to Hungary: "We are all working in full accord . . . and are doing all we can. But speedy assistance is sometimes physically impossible." The word "sometimes" in Lenin's communiqué could be taken sarcastically, since the month of July was almost over and, by then, Hungary's republic of soviets was already collapsing.[18]

11

Germany and Russia Resume Relations

The general public in the Western countries continued to think Lenin was trying to promote proletarian revolution as soon as possible everywhere, but statesmen and politicians in those countries had already realized that his aims were not as they appeared. The public was slow to grasp the situation because people were blinded by their passions, while men in government, used to making calculated political decisions, perceived that Lenin, too, had to make his choices based on similar calculation. No one knew this better than the government of Germany. Since 1917, the Germans had been in a position to observe Lenin's pragmatism and unscrupulousness. In 1918, they had established diplomatic relations with the Bolshevik government and had reached wide-ranging accords with it. Although at the end of 1918 the Berlin government decided to interrupt relations with Moscow, the sole purpose of this decision was to placate and reassure the Entente powers, which were preparing to dictate their conditions for peace.

The period of crisis in Russian-German relations did not last long. By the spring and summer of 1919, Berlin was already considering the possibility of reopening the dialogue with Moscow. The most convinced promoters of this reconciliation were the German chiefs of staff of the armed forces, who felt indignant about the harsh peace conditions imposed by the Allies on their nation and its army. *Rapprochement* between the two countries could be explained further by commonly shared predicaments. Both Germany and Russia had reasons to be upset over what had been decided (and what had not been decided) by the Treaty of Versailles. Both nations looked apprehensively on the building of a new Poland which, thanks to the new international order, was now situated right between the two nations.

Analyzing Russian-German relations, Winston Churchill expressed his growing feelings of alarm during a meeting of Entente delegates in Paris on

15 February 1919. He asserted that while the German state might not be an immediate danger, in five or ten years it would surely regain its power if it succeeded in allying itself with Russia — no matter if it were Bolshevik or non-Bolshevik Russia.[1] Subsequently, on 25 March, Lloyd George gave several delegates of the Entente in Paris a secret memorandum that spoke of the risks involved in a possible Russian-German alliance:

> The greatest danger that I see in the present situation is that Germany may throw in her lot with Bolshevism and place her resources, her brains, her vast organizing power at the disposal of the revolutionary fanatics whose dream it is to conquer the world for Bolshevism by force of arms. This danger is no mere chimera.[2]

The following day, President Wilson's chief aide, Colonel House, told Italian Prime Minister Orlando that if the Allies did not make peace with the Soviets, they surely would come to an agreement with Germany.[3] It is evident that the Western statesmen considered the Soviet state one of the great powers and did not believe that it was destined to remain in permanent segregation because of its Bolshevik government.

Among the Germans, the most influential promoter of agreement with the Soviets was General Hans von Seeckt, creator and head of the new German army. Von Seeckt was part of the inner circle of political decision-making in the Weimar Republic. As historian Edward H. Carr has noted, General von Seeckt became convinced in the year 1919 that the Bolsheviks, who had already been in power for almost two years, were likely to remain in power for several years longer; consequently, it seemed to him wise to have them as friends.[4] Carr has pointed out that the general was perhaps the first German leader to feel that there was "nothing incompatible" about being anti-Bolshevik in domestic politics and pro-Bolshevik in foreign politics.[5] In January 1920, the general set down this theory in a memorandum in which he spoke of accord with Soviet Russia as one of Germany's "immovable" goals. He was convinced that such agreement would be strengthened by the hostility of both countries toward Poland:

> I refuse to support Poland even in the face of the danger that she may be swallowed up. On the contrary, I count on that; and, even if we cannot at the moment help Russia to re-establish her former imperial frontiers, we certainly should not hinder her.[6]

During 1919, Von Seeckt and others persuaded the German government to make several friendly gestures toward Lenin's Russia. The first of these, in August, was to order the anti-Bolshevik *Freikorps* (irregular troops) to pull back from the Baltic regions.[7] In October came the second gesture of friendship, when Germany refused to join in the anti-Soviet blockade proposed by the Allies. The discussion which took place in the Reichstag revealed that across the whole political spectrum parliamentarians wanted to improve relations with Russia, and not one of them came out in favor of the blockade.[8]

The third sign of friendship that autumn consisted of an exchange of "messengers," after the break in diplomatic relations that had occurred a year earlier. The Bolsheviks sent to Berlin Viktor Kopp, a representative of the Office of the Commissar for Foreign Affairs.[9] The Germans assigned to Moscow Turkish General Enver Pasha, ex-Minister of War and Supreme Commander of the Turkish Army during the First World War. At the end of 1918, Enver Pasha had taken refuge in Berlin with his ex-chief of staff who, not very surprisingly, was General von Seeckt. In fact, during World War I, a number of German officers had fought together with the Turks, and these two generals had worked side by side.[10]

Enver Pasha left Berlin for Moscow on 10 October 1919, in a Junkers aircraft. The plane was forced to land in Kovno, Lithuania, where British soldiers stationed in that city took him into custody, along with the other passengers. Apparently, the British did not recognize Enver Pasha, but they did confiscate two interesting documents. The first was a map, dated 1 September 1919 and drawn up by the German General Staff, with important information about the military forces that might be mobilized against the Soviet state in countries hostile to it. The second was a letter written by the Junkers Aircraft Company to the Soviets, containing a proposal to work jointly in the aeronautical sector. (Some time later, Junkers was one of the first German firms to draw up contracts of cooperation with the Soviets.)[11] Subsequently, through the help of a German officer close to von Seeckt, Enver Pasha managed to escape from Lithuania and reach Moscow. The Soviet government put him up in a mansion, opposite the Kremlin, normally used to house very important foreign visitors.[12]

Meanwhile, the Bolshevik envoy to Germany, Viktor Kopp, arrived in Berlin at the end of October and was received by German Chancellor Müller on three successive occasions (1 November and 1 and 27 December).[13] German newspapers of the day repeatedly printed the view that in the future their government was going to have to place its trust in Russia.[14] Kopp, in the name of his government, urged that Russia and Germany establish regular political and commercial relations. Berlin, however, was hesitant, knowing that a renewal of normal relations between the two countries was bound to irritate the Allies.

By 20 February 1920, Kopp had succeeded in getting himself fully accredited as the representative of Soviet Russia in Germany. The Berlin government, in turn, chose a diplomat named Gustav Hilger, probably the best versed in Russian affairs in the German diplomatic corps, to represent it in Moscow.[15] The day before, General von Seeckt, speaking in Hamburg, announced frankly that the future of Germany lay in cooperating with Russia.[16]

12

Radek's "Political Salon"

The Soviets had another representative in Germany during the year 1919 who, though he had no official standing, was more important in many ways than Viktor Kopp. It was the Bolshevik leader Karl Radek, whom Lenin had sent there in November 1918.[1]

Radek had arrived in Germany secretly in the guise of a former German war prisoner. On 12 February 1919, he was discovered and imprisoned. But the conditions of Radek's imprisonment were unique. The prisoner was made so comfortable that, as he himself later admitted, it was as if he were playing host to a "political salon."[2] The Germans knew him well, since he had been part of the Russian delegation to the Brest-Litovsk negotiations the year before. Upon his arrest, the German government decided to treat him as a respected guest, a representative of the Soviet state with which it might establish long-lasting cooperative relations in the very near future.

In his Berlin prison-salon Radek received many important people, and one of the first was Enver Pasha:

> Two of my first guests were the former Grand Vizier Talaat Pasha, the head of the Young Turk government, and his War Minister Enver Pasha, the hero of the defence of Tripoli. After the rout of Turkey, they lived semi-illegally in Berlin — the Entente was demanding their extradition — and they were planning how to conduct the further defence of Turkey. Enver, having fled after the rout through Soviet Russia illegally to Germany, was the first to bring home to the German militarists that Soviet Russia was a new and growing world force on which they would have to count if they in fact meant to struggle against the Entente.[3]

Talaat Pasha and Enver Pasha told Radek that the Muslim world would be able to win its freedom only through the support of its own masses and that of the Soviet state. Radek sought to persuade the two Turkish leaders to visit Russia as soon as possible. In fact, Enver Pasha left for Russia in October 1919.

Among the personalities Radek received in his "political salon" was Walter Rathenau, the head of the electrical appliance company AEG, who had skillfully organized the German economy during World War I, and was to become Minister of Foreign Affairs. Rathenau expressed the view that proletarian Russia would not be defeated; the peasants would never permit the return of the big landowners, and the bourgeoisie was destined to remain as weak as it had always been. Even a well-known intellectual named Maximilian Harden paid a visit to Radek in prison. Harden's opinion was that it would be absurd for Germany to ignore the enormous force of Soviet Russia. Another visitor was Baron Eugen Freiherr von Reibnitz, the head of German "national Bolshevism," a movement that aimed to give the German state its former role as a great power by nationalizing its industries and allying itself with Lenin. When Radek got out of prison in November 1919, he stayed at von Reibnitz's home until he left the country.

The long list of important people Radek met in Berlin included, significantly, leaders of Germany's rightists. Colonel Max Bauer, former head of the Secret Services under General Ludendorff's Supreme Command, told him that, at the opportune moment, the German military might come to an accord with the Communist party and Lenin's Russia in order to carry out a coup d'état in Berlin. Commodore Paul von Hintze, ex-Minister of Foreign Affairs, who had helped draw up the Treaty of Berlin with the Bolsheviks in 1918, informed Radek that he endorsed the idea of arriving at further agreements with them.[4]

Karl Radek was permitted regular and frequent contact with representatives of the Left. One of these, the young revolutionary Ruth Fischer, recorded her experience in her memoirs. She described how surprised she had been when she discovered the privileged condition of Radek's imprisonment. Fischer was accompanied on her visit by a Swiss socialist called Karl Moor, who took her first to General von Seeckt's office, where all doors opened for them. There, an officer of the General Staff handed her a false identity card and, thanks to this pass, the young woman was granted permission to enter Radek's prison three times a week.[5]

Radek maintained a very consistent approach toward the German revolutionaries. At every opportunity he repeated that Germany was not ready for revolution and that the taking of power by the German proletariat was unimaginable. When the Berliners were on the point of insurrection on 6 January 1919, Radek had come out resolutely against it.[6] Two days before his arrest in February, he had addressed a letter to the German communists expressing his skepticism about the imminence of revolution throughout Europe:

As I have often written in the Russian press, and as I told you in my lectures, I am convinced that the development of the revolution in Western Europe will be slow because of the strength and organization of the bourgeoisie and because the proletariat lacks revolutionary allies, such as the peasants were in Russia.[7]

On 13 March 1919, Radek wrote a revealing letter from his "prison-salon" to French writer Alphonse Paquet, in which he not only reiterated his skepticism, but also passed an extremely negative judgment on the German Left: "Germany lacks a large revolutionary party. The communists are basically a party of cadres, not a real party with a tradition behind it, as we were in Russia in 1917." The German proletariat had always been fighting for reforms within the existing order. Therefore, according to Radek, "the organizations inherited by the German working class stood side by side with the bourgeoisie, constituting the basis for a counter-revolution." He did not go so far as to predict that the possibility of German revolution was forever excluded, but he pointed out all the internal and international conditions that made revolution improbable, while making a process of gradual reforms the more likely road for Germany.[8]

Contrary to the moderate and gradual perspective, however, in April 1919, Bavarian revolutionaries rose up in revolt and proclaimed the establishment of a republic of soviets in Munich. There is documental proof that the Communist Central Committee had sent out directives advising against this insurrection. One of them read: "In all frankness and with every emphasis the workers must be told that they should forgo any kind of armed action, even when a local or momentary success might be possible."[9] When the revolt took place, the Central Committee ordered the Bavarian communists to "liquidate" their soviet experiment immediately.[10]

The Bavarian soviets had been sending cordial and friendly messages to Bolshevik Russia since 7 April, but Lenin waited until 27 April to reply. His answer had such a condescending tone and included so many and unrealistic short-term objectives, that it seemed as if his intention was to provoke self-doubt, if not dismay.[11] Radek disclosed the reasons for the Bolshevik caution in an open letter to the German communists who were gathered in Heidelberg for their congress. Underlining the following words, he wrote:

Unless world revolution occurs sooner than indications appear up to now, the problem for Soviet Russia's foreign politics, along with that of all the other countries in which the working class is victorious, lies in arriving at a "modus vivendi" with the capitalist states. . . . The possibility of peace between capitalist countries and proletarian states is not utopic.[12]

It would be a mistake to think that because Radek had been in Berlin about a year by then, he was in any way isolated from his party or uninformed about the latest developments in Lenin's policies. Since the arrival of Viktor Kopp in Berlin in October 1919, Radek had met with him more than once, and their meetings provided him with an excellent source of information on events in Moscow. As the prisoner himself recorded, "from Kopp I learned in detail about the situation in Russia, and received papers and new Russian books."[13] Hence, the views he passed on to the German communists were given with full knowledge of the current situation.

In November, Radek helped the two most important German communist leaders, Paul Levi and Clara Zetkin, to write the tactical directives of the Comintern for Western Europe. The premise underlying these directives was that revolution on a European scale would be "a long process." After Radek returned to Moscow, he was criticized, but not by Lenin, for his pessimistic outlook. His critic was Bukharin, whom Lenin accused of suffering from hallucinations, precisely because of his views on world revolution.[14] When Radek was leaving Germany for Russia in January 1920, he granted the *Manchester Guardian* an illuminating interview in which he made the following remarks:

> It is the standpoint of the Russian government that normal and good relations are just as possible between socialist and capitalist states as they have been between capitalist and feudal states. For example, imperialist England lived on quite good terms with czarist feudal Russia in the days of serfdom. I, personally, am convinced that communism can only be saved through good relations with the capitalist states.[15]

Once back in Russia, Radek was named Secretary of the Comintern — Lenin's reward to him. In his first public address, on 28 January, he repeated the ideas he had been championing for months:

> If our capitalist partners abstain from counter-revolutionary activities in Russia, the Soviet government, too, will abstain from promoting revolutionary activities in capitalist countries. . . . We think that now capitalist countries can live alongside a proletarian State. We hold that it is in the interests of both sides to make peace and establish commercial relations.[16]

13

Lenin and the Italian Revolutionaries

In 1919, it might have seemed that Italy was on the verge of revolution. In the streets many were shouting to "do what they did in Russia." The Italian Socialist party announced in October that it had joined the Comintern. On 28 October 1919, as soon as Lenin received word of its membership, he addressed a letter "to comrade Serrati and to all Italian communists" — a letter that brought to light what his actual projects were.[1]

Lenin began his message by confessing that he did not know very much about what was happening in Italy. Nonetheless, he urged his Italian comrades not to make any moves. Evidently, his motivation had to do with the situation internationally and within Russia, since he admittedly was not aware of the Italian events. "Britain and France," he wrote, "with the cooperation of the Italian bourgeoisie, may possibly try to provoke the Italian proletariat to a premature uprising in order the easier to crush it. But their provocation will fail." To counteract the risk of revolution being "premature," the Italian communists were to win "the entire industrial and the *entire rural* proletariat plus the small peasants" to the communist cause. This meant, of course, about 90 percent of the entire working population. In other words, the Bolshevik leader was setting impossible conditions before authorizing Italian communists to seize power. Furthermore, he added that the revolution in Italy should take place only "after the proper moment is chosen internationally." This was tantamount to saying that the Italian Socialist party was to leave that decision to the Comintern, the international organization it had just joined. But the Comintern was against an insurrection, as Lenin's letter made clear.

Angelica Balabanova, who worked in the secretariat of the Comintern, read the letter before it was sent off. She was so struck by its content that she telephoned Lenin to say that his message risked being badly misinterpreted. "It will play into the hands of the opponents," she pointed out, "since it is they who claim that Italy is not ready for revolution." Lenin took his letter back, re-read it, and quickly returned it to Balabanova with instructions not to alter even a comma of the text. He apparently was not afraid of playing into the hands of the anti-revolutionaries.[2]

Lenin's message was interpreted by the Italians exactly as Balabanova had foreseen. It was printed in the socialist newspaper *Avanti!* on 6 December 1919, and caused considerable dismay. Scholar and politician Gaetano Salvemini remarked that it "was widely considered a cold shower that Lenin had poured over the heads of Italian extremists."[3] The nationalistic rightists suspected the letter was false, since it seemed quite improbable that Lenin would have imparted such cautious instructions.[4] A few months later, a socialist member of Parliament, Cesare Alessandri, wrote that Italian socialism had been transformed by the affair. Until then, as he put it, they thought they had to have "a ballot in one hand and a rifle in the other"; from then on, "we treasured Lenin's strangely procrastinating advice and we repeated our old proverb, '*chi va piano va sano e va lontano*' ['Slow and steady wins the race']."[5]

Serrati, the most authoritative leader of Italian socialism at the time, reassured Lenin that there would not be any reckless moves in Italy. "Neither sudden attack nor excessive delay," he told Lenin, "In my opinion, that is what our tactics should be. We have to work and wait patiently. Events will come to a head for us."[6] Italian socialism was later faulted for these delaying tactics which contributed considerably to the movement's downfall. But at that time the tactics evidently corresponded to Lenin's wishes.

Karl Radek, who was still in Germany in December 1919, learned of Lenin's letter to the Italians and used it to restrain all those outside of Italy who were showing signs of revolutionary impatience. Radek had already managed to coax the German Communist party into a more moderate position, but he was having trouble persuading the Austrians to do the same. Lenin's message to Serrati helped him beat down their last signs of resistance. "Thanks only to the appearance in *Avanti!* of a letter by Vladimir Ilyich to the Italian socialists expressing the sense in which I acted," Radek wrote, "was it possible to convince the Austrian Central Committee."[7]

Italian socialists later received other communications from the Bolsheviks advising against revolt. In February 1920, for instance, *Avanti!* printed an appeal signed by two clandestine representatives of the Comintern in Italy, W. Degot and Elena Sokolovska. The appeal contained two requests which, in the months to come, would cause bitter controversy among Italian socialists. The first was to fight actively against the reformist factions; the second was to change the name of the party from "socialist" to "communist." Degot and Sokolovska did not advocate a clash with the bourgeoisie, however. They recommended "beginning a revolutionary construction," but these beginnings were to be limited to "propaganda." The two mentioned the setting up of soviets only very generically. Their most important request to their Italian comrades was to encourage Italy's government as well as the bourgeoisie to recognize the Soviet republic and to visit Russia, where "doors would be opened wide" to them.[8]

Italian Prime Minister Francesco Saverio Nitti was a politician of keen intellect who accurately sized up the situation. He endorsed a foreign policy that was decidedly cordial toward Soviet Russia, for reasons of both domestic and international politics. It can be stated that Nitti pursued his "pro-Bolshevism" as far as Italy's international alliances and domestic public opinion permitted. On 7 February 1920, the same day *Avanti!* published Degot and Sokolovska's appeal, the Prime Minister pronounced the following words in the Chamber of Deputies:

> The invitation extended to me to resume economic relations with Russia does not leave me indifferent.
> I do not harbor the illusions that some of us have regarding conditions in Russia, and particularly about the existence of huge reserves of food; but no matter. For all the peoples of Europe, renewed relations with Russia is of prime importance, and this is especially true for Italy because of its geographic position, its deficiency in foreign trade and its shortage of means of mercantile transport. I have already made great efforts in this direction. . . . I am convinced that there will be a moderating influence on Russian governments as a result of their entering into direct relations with the rest of Europe after this period of isolation is over. I believe it is in our best interests, more than any other country's, to re-establish these relations as soon as possible.[9]

The Nitti government's pro-Soviet policy was very well received by the socialists. But even among anti-socialists it did not meet with opposition. *Idea Nazionale*, published by the Italian nationalistic factions, declared that the government should recognize the Soviet state "in order to assert its independence from the hegemonic powers" that had attempted to humiliate Italy at the Paris peace conference. It also stated that raw materials imported from Russia would give the nation "the best means of avoiding the economic-political blackmail" perpetrated by these same powers.[10]

On 13 December 1919, the Italian Chamber of Deputies voted down a socialist proposal to resume diplomatic relations with Moscow immediately.

But at the same time, it unanimously approved a motion to recognize all governments existing de facto in the ex-czarist empire, including also the Soviet government:

> The Chamber resolves that our government urge, in the Council of the Entente, the abandonment of all intervention in Russian internal affairs, the end of the blockade, and the resumption of diplomatic and commercial relations with all the de facto governments that have been set up since the fall of the czarist empire.[11]

The Bolsheviks reacted very enthusiastically to this motion and they made known how much hope they placed in Italian diplomacy. On 31 December, Chicherin sent the following telegram to Italy's Minister of Foreign Affairs:

> Having learned by wireless of the Italian Chamber's resolution regarding the resumption of relations with Soviet Russia and the Italian government's declarations along the same lines, the Soviet government of Russia warmly welcomes these decisions which are in the true interests of both peoples. . . . The Soviet government proposes to the Italian government to resume relations between the two nations immediately.[12]

It was clear that Chicherin had considerably exaggerated the scope of the motion passed by the Italian Chamber of Deputies, not for lack of information, but rather out of political expediency. (Chicherin and Lenin both knew that the socialists' proposal for immediate recognition of Soviet Russia had not passed). His purpose was threefold: to encourage Nitti's government in its diplomatic policy, to urge Italy to lead the way for the other powers, and to make it known to all that the Italians were taking the right road.[13]

Nitti felt he was on the right road regarding his control over the situation in Italy. At the end of December, his announcement to the international press showed how totally sure he felt about Italy's political stability: "I am absolutely certain that, if there is any country in the world where there should be no fears of impending revolution, that country is Italy." There had been and would continue to be local insurrectional movements, but in the Prime Minister's judgment, there was an abyss between these local events and a generalized revolutionary movement.[14]

At that time, a good number of Italian socialists were voicing similar opinions. On 31 January 1920, Serrati explained in a letter to Austrian communist leader Karl Toman that "the situation in Italy is not what some of you believe it to be. The whole movement of discontent here burns itself out in local skirmishes. The elections, together with a few large scale strikes, have acted as a sort of safety valve in letting off steam." Then, in order not to overly demoralize his Austrian comrade, Serrati added: "This does not mean that a movement could no longer be organized; it simply means that more time is definitely needed."[15] One month later, the *Manchester Guardian* published an interview in which Filippo Turati confirmed the view that "the revolutionary peril is not such as to cause undue anxiety in Italy." According to Turati, the left wing of the Socialist party was fanning the fire of Soviet theories only to keep the masses awake and excited, but such theories were totally impracticable. The Left promoted continuous agitations only "to delay the moment when the working classes will lose their illusions and faith in their cherished myths."[16]

Many historians, analyzing events in Italy after the First World War, have exaggerated both the mirage of the revolutionaries and the fears of the conservatives, but the facts indicate that most politicians and statesmen kept themselves far away from either of these extremes. Prime Minister Nitti, in particular, had enough first-hand information to make an accurate evaluation of the situation. In the spring of 1920, an informer by the name of Francesco Perri who resided in Switzerland and kept in touch with the Bolsheviks, sent the central headquarters of the Italian police a report that quite aptly summarized Lenin's foreign policy:

> The socialists in Western countries are fooling themselves into believing that the Russian Bolsheviks are aiming to bring revolution to Western Europe. Lenin, Trotsky, Krasin and their collaborators are using the Western socialists to achieve their own goals of creating a Russia that is great, strong, powerful and free from any commitment to Western Europe. The threat of spreading revolution beyond Russia, along with the other Bolshevik propaganda abroad, is just meant to intimidate, in order to convince the Entente nations to recognize the Soviet government and resume commercial, political and diplomatic relations with Bolshevik Russia, as they had with czarist Russia. In the nations that have agreed to deal with the Soviets, the Russians have been abstaining from all forms of propaganda. Where a Bolshevik representative office does exist in these countries (such as in Amsterdam), it is operated exclusively for purposes of propaganda in countries inimical to the Soviets.
> Russian Bolsheviks are purer and more intransigent nationalists than those who oppose them in the name of fatherland and order.[17]

Another document, even more convincing than Perri's report, was sent to Rome by the Italian naval attaché in Stockholm, Manfredi Gravina, in April 1920. During one of several conversations he had with Soviet diplomat Maksim Litvinov, Gravina had asked the Russian if he really considered revolution in Italy opportune, for the good of the people:

> Litvinov's answer was as follows: We know quite well that a revolution would not be expedient in Italy today. The result would be an immediate declaration by France of a blockade — perhaps even a declaration of war. It would serve the purposes of French capitalism and imperialism, and this is certainly not what we want. Whatever our influence may count for, we in Moscow have been continuously advising against revolution in Italy.[18]

Lenin, too, maintained that "in the event of the proletariat's victory in Italy, blockade of that country by Great Britain, France and America is possible and probable."[19] And in her memoirs, Angelica Balabanova recounted a conversation she had with Lenin in September 1920, while Italian workers were occupying factories:

> When I was about to say goodbye [Lenin] casually mentioned the news that had just been received from Italy: "the occupation of the factories" and the peasants' demonstrations. Lenin showed no enthusiasm over the news. When he asked my opinion I replied: "If you want to know what I think of the latest developments, I do not know any more than you do; we have both read the same news. But if you are referring to the general situation in Italy, I can only say that in no other European country are the masses so ready for social revolution and for socialism as in Italy."
>
> "For social revolution?" he repeated in an irritated tone. "But don't you know that Italy lacks natural resources? Don't you think about bread and coal? No, we do not want a repetition of the Hungarian defeat." And he went on enumerating the fatal consequences a revolution in Italy would bring at that time.[20]

Two years later, Zinoviev publicly confirmed that in 1920 the Comintern had not asked the Italians to start a revolution, for fear of a Hungarian-type failure. As Zinoviev explained it, all that was asked of the Italians was to prepare the party to make revolution at some future time.[21]

14
Bolshevism and Asia

When the Bolshevik state took the place of the czarist regime, the vast empire it inherited stretched from Europe to Asia. In creating history's first socialist state, the Bolsheviks were the protagonists of an extraordinary and grandiose revolutionary event that made an impression reaching far beyond the borders of the old czarist empire. It was therefore quite natural for Lenin to devise his policies on a world scale, making a concentrated effort to fit any opportunities that arose into a general and consistent global design. The opportunities Asia offered him were part of this inclusive plan; indeed, they were an essential part.

The importance of Asia was most apparent in regard to Anglo-Russian relations. During the czarist era, Great Britain and Russia had competed for territory in Asia, to such an extent that many thought actual war might break out between the two empires. The Russian revolution of 1905 aroused new fears among the British, since it could serve as a model for the Asians to follow. This revolution had demonstrated that constitutional guarantees could be obtained even in an autocratic, agrarian state whose population belonged to the Asian family of peoples and was largely illiterate.[1]

The 1917 revolution proved much more than that, conferring on the Russian insurgents even greater authority and prestige, aside from the effects produced by their arsenals and financial means. The Bolshevik government then proceeded to carry out operations in Asia which provoked agitation and rebellion. Lenin reasoned that the survival of the Soviet state could be guaranteed by virtue of the fact that it posed a considerable threat to the British empire. Carefully gauging this menace might induce the British to compromise with Moscow. As far back as December 1917, Lenin and his Commissar for Nationalities, Stalin, issued a proclamation whose purpose was to incite all Muslims to insurrection against their oppressors.[2] In January 1918, a Soviet republic of Turkestan was established, and in the following November the First Congress of Muslim Communists was organized in Moscow in order to intensify propaganda efforts in the Orient.[3]

The Bolsheviks became even more active in Asia in 1919, attempting to extend their influence to Afghanistan and Persia with the eventual goal of getting as far as India.[4] By the summer of 1919, some Bolshevik leaders considered Asia to be more vital than Europe in pursuing their political ends. On 5 August, for instance, just a few days after the defeat of Bela Kun's Hungarian republic, Trotsky sent a secret note to the Bolshevik Central Committee urging a radical change in foreign policy. He was convinced that the revolutionary movement should shift toward the Orient, and pointed out that a revolutionary body in Asia might take on greater importance than the European-dominated Comintern. He proposed setting up an academy to educate and prepare political and military personnel for the Asian revolutionary struggle, and he added that the Red Army was opening the way to India.[5]

In August, Chicherin published an article reminding his comrades that as far back as 1856, a czarist minister of foreign affairs, Prince Gorchakov, had stated that Russia's future lay in Asia. Chicherin asserted that now, in the proletarian era, the historic unity of the Russian and Asian masses would be able to express itself in united anti-imperialist action.[6] During the same summer, Zinoviev ordered Angelica Balabanova to stop dealing with European affairs and to go to Turkestan. When she asked the reason for this transfer, Zinoviev replied, "Because our whole policy has turned towards the Orient; it is of utmost importance to us."[7]

Lenin, who attributed an essential role to Asia, in a speech to the Second All-Russia Congress of Communist Organizations of the Peoples of the East (held in Moscow in November–December 1919), reiterated that the objective should be to provoke revolutionary activities among the Orientals. He did not maintain that the Asians were ready for socialism, however. He declared, instead, that they were to fight "against the medieval survivals" (therefore not against Capital). Indeed, he openly admitted that uprisings in the Orient had little to do with Marxism: "Such are the problems whose solution you will not find in any communist book." He recognized that it would not be the proletariat but the bourgeoisie that would lead these revolts. "You will have to base yourselves on bourgeois nationalism," he said to the insurgents.[8]

At the Second Congress of the Comintern held in Moscow in July–August 1920, when Lenin repeated the concept that insurrection by the colonized peoples had to be encouraged even at the expense of being led by the local petty bourgeoisie, many of the European communists were dumbfounded. They simply could not understand how Lenin could favor the Asian bourgeoisie and yet be hostile toward the socialist reformists of Europe. Even some Asian communists expressed their doubt and opposition. An Indian representative M.N. Roy, who was highly respected in the Comintern, disagreed strongly with Lenin's ideas, objecting to any alliances, even temporary ones, with the petty bourgeoisie of the colonial countries. He was convinced that revolution in Asia was not then possible. Lenin took up the debate with Roy, passionately affirming that backward countries, with the help of the proletariat of advanced countries, could progress to a Soviet system and achieve communism without passing through the capitalist phase.[9]

Lenin contended that it would be wise to adopt tactics in Asia that differed from those applied in Europe. First and foremost, in preindustrial Asia there were no workers' parties for them to count on. If the Bolsheviks wanted to put any kind of pressure on local governments or the British empire, they had little choice but to ally themselves with the local bourgeois nationalists. Secondly, the Soviet state, though it was directly responsible for the behavior of European communists, had much more limited responsibility for the actions of the Asian bourgeoisie. Thirdly, while a successful socialist revolution in any industrial European country could easily usurp the revolutionary primacy of the Bolsheviks, and perhaps even their power, the success of a bourgeois revolution in the Orient would not have the same consequence.

Evidently, Lenin intended to proceed cautiously in Asia. His aim was to exploit the revolutionary bourgeoisie so as to influence Asian governments, with the ultimate aim of resuming political and commercial ties with other nations. This would help guarantee Soviet security and make it possible to use the governments of those nations in his diplomatic struggles with the West. Lenin's policies, then, were clearly dominated by an extremely pragmatic approach toward Asia.

Events in Persia well illustrate Lenin's tactics. During the First World War, Persia had been occupied by both czarist and British troops. After the Bolshevik Revolution, the British invaded the Russian zone of influence and advanced all the way to Baku, using Persian bases for operations against the Red Army. In the spring of 1920, the Bolsheviks attacked the British, bombing and occupying the Caspian Sea port of Enzeli, invading the province of Gilan, and forcing the British to pull back toward the south. The Shah, who had been far from happy about the British occupation, was quite satisfied with this turn of events, and Persia's consultative assembly even found the courage to refuse ratification of a treaty with Great Britain.[10]

The Soviets, however, permitted a Persian national progressive movement to set up a socialist republic in Gilan. This awakened fears in the Teheran government, and the Persians sent a diplomatic mission to Moscow to discuss the matter with the Bolsheviks and come to some sort of agreement. The Soviets then gradually withdrew their support of Gilan's socialist republic. On 22 October 1920, the Central Executive Committee of Persia's Communist party proclaimed that its country was not ready for socialism, since it had to pass through the democratic-bourgeois phase first. In February 1921, the Persian Minister of War, Reza Khan (who was later to become Shah), carried out a successful coup d'état and formed a new government. Moscow, in opening friendly relations with Reza Khan and permitting him to do away with the socialist republic of Gilan, offered an excellent demonstration of Lenin's instrumentalism in regard to Persia's revolutionary movement.[11]

In Afghanistan the Bolsheviks immediately inaugurated excellent relations with Emir Amanullah, who came to power in February 1919. One of Amanullah's first gestures was to recognize Lenin's government and to send an Afghan-Indian delegation to Moscow, since he, too, was anxious to throw off British hegemony. The Bolsheviks, in turn, recognized the Emir's government while a war was being fought between the Afghans and the British in May 1919. The first ambassador from Afghanistan arrived in Moscow in October and was solemnly received by Soviet authorities, including Lenin himself. *Izvestiia*, on 14 October 1919, announced that M. Sultan-Galiev, representing the Soviet government, complimented the new ambassador on how "small but heroic Afghanistan" was struggling to free itself from centuries-old British oppression. The Soviets, on their part, sent an ambassador to Kabul, and soon the Afghan capital became an important meeting-place for Bolsheviks and Indian rebels.[12]

Finally, events in Turkey serve as further proof that Lenin's ultimate goal was to arrive at agreement with other governments, not to promote revolutions. The Turkish Communist party was founded in the fall of 1920 under the leadership of Mustafa Sufi, a revolutionary who had lived in Russia. The party's activities, however, quickly aroused the hostility of Kemal Pasha's government. Kemal Pasha did not exclude the possibility of accords with Lenin, but at the same time, did not want his country disturbed by internal communist activity. He therefore promoted the establishment of an "official" Communist party (called the Kesmi), having no direct relations with Moscow, that had a party platform stating that Turkey was not ready for communism.

Sixteen leaders of Turkey's Communist party and friends of Moscow, including Mustafa Sufi, were slain in January 1921. The Turkish government denied having ordered the massacre, but the denial did not sound convincing. All this, however, did not prevent the Soviets from signing a friendship treaty with the government of Turkey a few weeks later. The treaty included mention of the "solidarity that exists between the two countries in the struggle against imperialism." Meanwhile, inside Turkey, members of Mustafa Sufi's party continued to be persecuted.[13]

15

London Fears the Russian Threat

Lenin was having difficulty opening the negotiations he so much wanted with the Allies. The Prinkipo conference never took place and the proposals given to William Bullitt received no answer, though Lenin confirmed their validity again and again. To help convince the Allies to negotiate, he brought into being a communist International which could create widespread unrest, especially in Asia. Furthermore, Moscow maintained special relations with Berlin, keeping the threat alive of a Russo-German accord against the Versailles treaty. Lastly, in order to feel more secure, Lenin assembled a large Red Army to defeat the White forces once and for all.

The Allies, meanwhile, were stalling for time, uncertain of what to do. They dared not negotiate officially with the Bolsheviks, but did not intend to go to war against them either. It was clear that the Versailles peace treaty would remain an essentially incomplete and unreliable document without the participation of the Russians; but the Allies still held the illusion that Lenin was on the verge of being overthrown by a combination of the White forces and economic turmoil. Once it became evident that the Red Army was defeating the Whites, the Allied nations realized they could no longer procrastinate, and, having excluded the possibility of war, they could only opt for peace.

British Prime Minister David Lloyd George decided to push for a peace arrangement that included Russia, which would be more secure and stable than the Treaty of Versailles. There were several reasons why Lloyd George, who had been showing an open mind toward the Bolsheviks for some time, resolved to foster this historically important policy switch. Political considerations within Britain led him to seek consensus from the Left by dealing with the new Russia. From an international standpoint, he was the head of an empire that was threatened by Russia in Asia. Restoration of the ex-czarist empire would have meant a return to the old problems in the Orient, while a permanently dismembered czarist empire and a weak Bolshevik Russia in its place might be the best solution. Hence, a new peace treaty that included such a Russia would give Great Britain more security. It would also assure the British Prime Minister much personal prestige. The negotiations that led to the Versailles accord had been dominated by President Wilson, who would not be attending a new peace conference for reasons of domestic politics as well as his precarious health. There would be no one who could steal the spotlight from Lloyd George.

The situation in Asia doubtless played a fundamental role in Britain's decisions. Winston Churchill had begun talking of the Bolshevik peril in Asia in March 1919. In June, Foreign Office Secretary Curzon wrote that a withdrawal of British troops from the Caucasus would give the Soviets the petroleum from Baku, the resources of Azerbaijan, and control over a vast area that stretched from the Black Sea to India. In September, Churchill repeated that the British government risked seeing all its interests in Afghanistan and Persia compromised.[1]

Nonetheless, the British along with the other Allies continued their military disengagement. Battalions were embarking at Archangel and Vladivostok for repatriation, while in September a Polish proposal to go to war with Russia was rejected. Allied leaders continued to meet in Paris, where the Prime Minister of a re-born Poland, Ignacy Jan Paderewski, secretly communicated that his nation was ready to deploy an army of 500,000 soldiers against the Russians, and asked the Allied powers to join in this undertaking. But, as E.M. Carroll has observed, the Allies were by then clearly heading toward very different solutions. The Americans were entering another period of isolationism; the French had decided on a policy of containment; the British and the Italians were oriented toward winding up interventionism in Russia.[2]

The British Prime Minister had no faith in the White armies. "I do not believe that Admiral Kolchak will defeat Lenin," he pronounced on 17 June 1919. At the end of September, he sent Churchill a letter explaining why no further assistance was to be given to the White forces. The White generals had fallen from grace:

> We have kept faith with all these men. But not a member of the Cabinet is prepared to go further. The various Russian enterprises have cost us this year between 100 and 150 million, when Army, Navy and Shipping are taken into account. Neither this government nor any other government that this country is likely to see will do more. We cannot afford it. The French have talked a good deal about anti-Bolshevism, but they have left it

to us to carry out the Allied policy. Clemenceau told me distinctly that he was not prepared to do any more. Foch is definitely opposed to these ventures at Allied expense. Their view is that our first duty is to clear up the German situation. I agree with them.[3]

Even though Churchill would have preferred to increase aid to the Whites, he was compelled to give in and propose a plan for a reduction in military expenses. The Allies could have continued the trade boycott, but by autumn 1919 it was becoming obvious that everyone wanted a resumption of trade. Many even maintained that resuming commercial exchange with the Soviets might itself cause the Bolsheviks' downfall, since they would not be able to compete economically.[4]

That autumn the Bolsheviks looked like the victors in the civil war; the Red Army chased Yudenich's troops from the outskirts of Petrograd and Denikin's army from Orel. This was a rather dismal state of affairs for the anti-Bolshevik crusaders. Meanwhile British MP Colonel Malone came back from Russia with the Soviets' conditions for peace. The proposals were almost exactly like those they had delivered to Bullitt a few months earlier. Malone outlined the conditions to the House of Commons on 5 November 1919.[5]

Lloyd George gave an important speech at London's Guildhall just three days later in which he publicly revealed his intention not to send further military aid to the Whites; he used arguments similar to those he had written in the September letter to Churchill. Great Britain, after having sent £100 million in aid, was no longer able to sustain the costs of the "interminable" civil war in Russia. He considered it indispensable to bring peace back to that nation, and since arms had proven inadequate to the task, other means had to be employed. The Prime Minister concluded with the hope that soon another opportunity might present itself to renew the invitation already extended to the Russians in January when the Prinkipo meeting had been proposed. Lloyd George's speech caused a sensation and stirred considerable protest. Both the *Times* of London and *Le Temps* printed criticisms of it.[6]

A few days later, when the Prime Minister took his case to the House of Commons, his speech received enthusiastic applause from Liberals and Laborites.[7] On 17 November, once again in the Commons, Lloyd George spoke of the need to thwart the Russian peril in Asia. He called up the memory of Disraeli who had seen a colossal, expanding Russia advance like an iceberg toward Persia and the borders of Afghanistan and India, and had considered it the greatest threat the British empire would face.[8]

During that same period the London government sent Labor MP James

O'Grady to Copenhagen to solve a humanitarian problem with the Soviets — the repatriation of war prisoners. This was the first formal contact ("semi-diplomatic") that an Allied power had had with Lenin's representatives in over a year.[9] Moscow had no intention of confining the talks to the sole question of prisoners. On 14 November, Maksim Litvinov received the assignment to negotiate peace between the states that succeeded the ex-czarist empire and the other countries — in other words, to come to a *modus vivendi* with the capitalist world.[10]

On 20 November, Chicherin made it known how much hope Lloyd George's policy was raising in Moscow:

> Relations with Russia are quite possible in spite of the profound differences between Britain's and Russia's régime. . . . The British customer and purveyor are as necessary to us as we are to them. Not only do we desire peace and the possibility of internal development, but we also feel strongly the need of economic help from the more fully developed countries such as Great Britain. We are ready even to make sacrifices for the sake of a close economic connection with Britain. . . . I, therefore, gladly welcome the declaration of the British Premier as the first step towards such a sane and real policy corresponding to the interests of both countries.[11]

The wishes Chicherin expressed, however, would not yet come true. While Lloyd George himself was "pro-Bolshevik," he was not free to carry out his policy. Liberals and Laborites supported him but the Conservatives, who were the strongest party in the coalition government, totally disagreed. Within the Entente, though the Italians encouraged the Prime Minister to deal with Lenin, the French were sending out signals to the contrary. In this climate of contrasting policies Lloyd George was forced to procrastinate. The situation was fluid, though; if cautious, one could take certain limited initiatives.

On 25 November 1919, the discussions between Litvinov and O'Grady got underway in Copenhagen. The Soviet envoy had received a broad mandate from Lenin. The British emissary, on the contrary, had received instructions from Foreign Secretary Curzon to deal only with the question of the prisoners.[12] France's ambassador to London began protesting even before the talks opened, claiming that O'Grady was about to discuss matters that went well beyond the prisoner issue, and the international press seemed to confirm this view.[13]

On the evening of the 29th, over an informal supper in a Copenhagen hotel, Litvinov told O'Grady that a formal peace proposal was going to be delivered to the Allies shortly. Ten days later, four sealed envelopes arrived at the Danish legation offices of the four Allies — Great Britain, France,

Italy, and the United States. The envelopes contained the resolution passed by the Congress of Soviets on 5 December. The Soviets began it by referring to all their previous peace initiatives, including the offers delivered to Bullitt. Then, they once again proposed an immediate opening of negotiations.[14]

The Allied legations refused to accept delivery of the envelopes, returning them without having broken the seals, with the explanation that they were not authorized to accept any official communications from the Soviet government. On 15 December, when Lloyd George reported this symbolic gesture to the House of Commons, he followed it up with a speech designed to reassure the Conservatives. He declared that peace with the Soviets would not be agreed upon until the Bolsheviks made peace with the Whites and restored democracy by holding free elections.

The Bolsheviks persevered in their efforts. Litvinov sent O'Grady a long letter on 22 December, in which he complained about Lloyd George's declarations and repeated the proposals for peace, including Soviet willingness to make concrete economic and political concessions. Bolshevik Russia was ready to forgo revolutionary propaganda:

> From the point of view of the vital interests of both countries there should be no obstacle to the establishment of real peace, excepting the bogey of revolutionary propaganda. If formal guarantees from the Soviet government on this point be considered insufficient, could not means of preventing this propaganda be devised without barring the way to mutual representation?[15]

It was essential to the British that revolutionary propaganda come to a stop in Asia. On 3 January 1920, Winston Churchill expressed alarm over "the ghost of the Russian bear" that roamed in regions leading to India.[16] Three days later, the British Foreign Secretary received an alarming message which said that Lenin, having given up on revolution in Europe, had decided to promote it in the Orient. The message came from Tbilisi and read as follows:

> Bolsheviks, having failed to upset Europe, have made agreements with Muslims to attack Great Britain. Both Turks and Bolsheviks have adopted this as a policy of despair. Lenin has taken [Kaiser] Wilhelm's place.[17]

Back in 1848, Marx and Engels had announced that the ghost of communism was roaming around Europe. At the beginning of 1920 it seemed that the ghost, which had fallen asleep in Europe, was waking up in Asia. The policy of the Bolsheviks consisted of holding out the promise of another long sleep, as long as the Soviet state was guaranteed its survival.

Karl Radek made the Soviets' designs very clear in an interview published by the *Manchester Guardian* on 8 January 1920. Radek, who was still in Berlin, knew how to alternate his statements between reassurances and threats. The newspaper's anonymous interviewer began by introducing Karl Radek to its readers as "one of Lenin's chief lieutenants, in regular communication with Moscow and entitled to speak with authority," and explained that the knowledge of world affairs Radek possessed was "almost a legend in Russia." It became evident that this was a well-founded legend when "he rapidly passed his finger over the map of Asia and in quick sentences described the local situations."

Radek, who appeared very sure of himself, asserted that the British press, speaking of the "Red menace to India," had exaggerated, mixing truths with falsehoods. The Orient was certainly in a state of turmoil, but the causes were autonomous and not artificially provoked by the Russians. Asian peoples were sending emissaries to the Russian capital, but, according to Radek, this was only natural. In 1905, as well, waves of revolution had extended from Russia to Asia. Moscow felt solidarity for the Asian peoples but did not have imperialistic designs. The Russians desired peace. In that case, the interviewer asked, what did he have to say about the Soviet threat in India through continued propaganda? Radek answered:

> The Russian government conducts no such propaganda. On the contrary, it is prepared to give to any country that establishes peaceful relations all conceivable guarantees. Of course, the march of ideas cannot be arrested, but we are ready to give guarantees that we shall use neither money nor agents, direct or indirect, for the conduct of propaganda in India as elsewhere in the British empire. We have too great [a] need for peace with England to haggle.

Radek expressed himself quite openly, going so far as to maintain that:

> British imperialism is not merely a capitalist intrigue, but is rooted in the psychology of the masses. The British domination of India and Ireland is popular. If we desire the British masses to become socialist, we cannot do anything from outside. Salvation must come to the English proletarians and oppressed people of the empire from their own exertions. It is their own affair, not that of the Soviet government. We can only offer our sympathy; anything further would be forbidden towards a country with which we were at peace.

At this point it was logical for the interviewer to ask if Soviet Russia really did intend to "settle down amid a non-socialist world as one state among others." This was Radek's reply:

Why not? It is the standpoint of the Russian government that normal and good relations are just as possible between socialist and capitalist states as they have been between capitalist and feudal states. For example, imperialist England lived on quite good terms with czarist feudal Russia in the days of serfdom. I, personally, am convinced that Communism can only be saved through good relations with the capitalist states. All the capitalist states are moving towards socialism along their own roads and in their varying degrees, and the pace will be quickened by the burden of war taxes and debt, high prices, and the lowered standard of living. But in each of these countries the battle will be won from within in the growing struggle between the peoples and governments. Revolutions never originate in foreign affairs but are made at home.

Radek claimed that the Soviet state was too weak "to indulge in a world policy or in a drive against India," but it was "strong enough to hurt in self defence." In any case, he said, Russia had no intention of exporting revolution at bayonet point:

> Let me refer to Lenin's statement at the last party congress in March 1919. "The sword is not the means by which the victory of communism is to be won." Such a policy of aggression would weaken us and our cause. Were we by action from outside to enable a revolutionary government to be set up in a country not strong enough to carry through a revolution itself, we should weaken ourselves by dispersing forces needed for our own defence.[18]

With careful doses of reassurance and threat, he made it understood that Soviet Russia was not going to forgo revolutionary propaganda in the Orient without receiving anything in return:

> But there is another side of the question. If we are forced to fight, naturally we seek a field of war where success is most easily attained. It is not true that we can do nothing; the Eastern door is open, and there are great possibilities. Had the old czarist government determined to advance on India it would have had to build railways, organize armies, accumulate supplies — in short, employ the resources of a capitalist *kultur*. With us it is quite different. All we have to do is to send out our most active workers to stir up unrest among populations. That is no new thing for Russians. You may remember the part played by Social Democrats from the Caucasus in the Persian Revolution of 1906 and later. I know personally quite a number of Caucasian comrades who were revolutionary leaders in Persia.
> What we can supply is the leadership so lacking in the East. We can send officers as instructors — not officers of the old school, but men of our own training, in particular artillery instructors who were formerly engineers in the Putilo Arsenal. These, the most intelligent artisans in Russia,

have the necessary mathematical knowledge to make first-rate artillery officers. We can send technical experts and can erect explosives factories and arsenals. And remember that when we proletarians send ten [hand-] picked men, after our experience of the last two years, it is equal to an expeditionary force. We are already in touch with the Young Turks by way of Tashkent, the Caspian and the Caucasian Azerbaijan. Young Turk officers whom I have recently met here in Berlin assure me that it would require fifteen divisions to dispose of the existing Turkish armies. Moreover, Asia Minor is already something of an international interracial powder magazine.[19]

After threatening, Radek concluded the long interview with a final, reassuring word whose purpose was to obtain what was most vital to Moscow — a peace settlement and the resumption of diplomatic relations with the West:

But there is no need to enlarge further on possibilities. Our crippled industries are paralyzed. Our historic task is to reconstruct Russia, and for that peace is essential. We are fighting simply because we are forced to do so, and are given no other choice. Russia is a democracy of peasants and workers [and will be so] for at least half a century to come. Your statesmen can count with certainty on the entire absence of capitalist imperialism in Russia. All the talk about our plans to disrupt and destroy the British empire is the sheerest nonsense and Northcliffe bluff.[20]

16
End of the Economic Blockade

At the close of 1919, the civil war in Russia was nearing its end, with the Red Army victorious. Yudenich's troops were defeated at the outskirts of Petrograd, Kolchak's soldiers suffered serious setbacks in the southern regions, and Denikin's forces were beaten at Orel and Voronezh. Since international policy depended strictly on the balance of power, the scales which had tipped in favor of Lenin's Russia brought still more power and greater prestige.

In December 1919, French Premier Georges Clemenceau announced that he wanted "to put a barbed wire fence around Bolshevism to prevent it from hurling itself on civilized Europe."[1] This declaration is still remembered today for its harsh tones. However, upon closer examination, it reveals an attitude that had become defensive rather than offensive. The "barbed wire fence" was no longer a war; it was a substitute for war. It was called upon as a last resort in order to protect capitalist Europe from the growing power of the Soviet state. The fence was also supposed to serve to contain the European bourgeoisie, which was seeking to revive friendly relations with the Soviets.

But the European ruling classes were no longer in the mood to listen to Clemenceau's warnings. British Prime Minister Lloyd George, in particular, was unwilling to listen any longer. Italian Prime Minister Francesco Saverio Nitti was another leader in favor of renewed political and commercial relations with Russia, but the real craftsman of the pro-Soviet policy at that time was Lloyd George. He directed Great Britain's policy toward Russia singlehandedly, at times differing openly with his Foreign Office Secretary, Curzon. By the closing days of 1919, Great Britain was negotiating with Maksim Litvinov in Copenhagen. Furthermore, important diplomatic negotiations were about to get underway in London at Number 10 Downing Street.

On 6 January 1920, the Entente nations revoked the "economic blockade" of Soviet Russia. This move showed how much the situation had been evolving in Lenin's favor. While both the British and Italian governments had been trying for some time to come to an agreement with Russia, the defeat of the Whites by the Red Army gave other Allied governments the opportunity to seek some kind of "normalcy" in Soviet relations. A halt to the economic boycott was also being called for in European economic circles, where many were anxious to buy raw materials from the Russians and, in turn, sell them machinery and manufactured goods. Removal of the blockade found its major justification in two coinciding hopes. First, resumption of trade between Soviet Russia and the rest of the world might lead to the transformation, perhaps even the demise, of Bolshevism. Second, once Russia was in communication with Western countries, the idealistic myths of Bolshevism could be swept away by the West. In order not to antagonize the diehard anti-Bolsheviks, though, the Supreme Council of the Allies announced that it intended to open up trade and commerce only with the "Russian cooperatives," and not with the Soviet government itself.

Lenin reacted quickly and firmly to the Allies' decision. He felt he was in a strong enough position to insist on a totally unequivocal accord. He also wanted to be sure that the Allies' decision would in no way undermine the Soviet system from within. To this purpose, the Bolshevik leader had a resolution passed by the Politburo of the Central Committee that immediately put all the cooperatives under a system of soviets.[2] A few days later, in an interview with American journalist Lincoln Eyre, correspondent for the *World*, Lenin announced this news and took the opportunity to repeat the fundamental goals of his foreign policy:

> All the world knows that we are prepared to make peace on terms the fairness of which even the most imperialistic capitalists could not dispute. We have reiterated over and over again our desire for peace, our need for peace and our readiness to give foreign capital the most generous concessions and guarantees. But we do not propose to be strangled to death for the sake of peace.
>
> I know of no reason why a socialistic commonwealth like ours cannot do business indefinitely with capitalistic countries. We don't mind taking their capitalistic locomotives and farming machinery, so why should they mind taking our socialistic wheat, flax and platinum? Socialistic corn tastes the same as any other corn, does it not?

Lenin emphasized that it would be in the interests of Western capitalists to be able to trade with the Soviets. At the same time, he did not try to hide the seriousness of Russia's economic situation:

> The statesmen of the Entente and the United States do not seem to understand that Russia's present economic distress is simply a part of the world's economic distress. . . . Without Russia, Europe cannot get on her feet. And with Europe prostrate, America's position becomes critical. . . . In Russia we have wheat, flax, platinum, potash and many minerals of which the whole world stands in desperate need. The world must come to us for them in the end, Bolshevism or no Bolshevism. There are signs that a realization of this truth is gradually dawning.

Along with this plan to resume international trade, Lenin explained that the Soviet state was looking at its future in terms of economic development, and he announced the well-known electrification program:

> We mean to electrify our entire industrial system through power stations in the Urals and elsewhere. Our engineers tell us it will take ten years. When the electrification is accomplished it will be the first important stage on the road to the communistic administration of public economic life.[3]

The *World* correspondent also interviewed Trotsky, who reiterated that the Bolsheviks, forced to defend themselves (successfully) against the Whites, ardently wished for peace. British and American aid was considered indispensable to set the transportation network on its feet again. According to Trotsky, his government was ready "to grant all possible guarantees to foreign capital invested in Russia, once a peace agreement had been signed."[4]

Within a few days it was clear that the Allies had accepted Lenin's decision and were getting ready to trade with the cooperatives that had been absorbed into the system of soviets. The Bolshevik leaders celebrated. They thought they had found in the cooperatives' soviet organization (*Centrosojuz*) a Trojan horse with which, finally, to get within the walls of Western diplomacy. Historian Louis Fischer has written: "For Moscow, this was one of the best jokes in ages, and years later Chicherin could not refrain from chuckle as he talked with me about it." But few people were deceived. Almost everybody in the West understood that dealing only with the cooperatives was a sham, but nobody worried excessively about it. The aim was to enter into relations with the new Soviet state, just as the Soviet government wanted to enter into peaceful relations with the rest of the world.[5]

On 2 February 1920, when Soviet Russia signed a peace treaty with Estonia, Lenin declared that it was an occasion of historic importance:

> This peace is a window into Europe. It opens up before us the possibility of

beginning an exchange of goods with the West. Our enemies maintained that the revolution in the West is far away and that we would not be able to hold out without it. We have not only held out, however, we have won a victory.[6]

Even *Le Temps* hailed the Bolshevik victories on the diplomatic front, but pointed out that Bolshevism was winning because it was betraying its theories. It was supposed to be proletarian, revolutionary, and internationalist. Instead, it was coming to agreement with the bourgeoisie, becoming despotic, restoring the old borders of Great Russia, dealing with capitalist governments and putting aside its plans for world revolution.[7]

By then all the Western countries felt that relations with Soviet Russia were entering a new, more calm and peaceful phase. On 10 February, Lloyd George told the House of Commons that the West was absolutely in no condition to fight a war and admitted that the White generals had failed to win theirs. Kolchak, captured by the Bolsheviks, had been shot by a firing squad three days earlier. Lloyd George stated:

> We have failed to restore Russia by force. I believe we can do it and save her by trade. Commerce has a sobering influence in its operations.... Trade, in my opinion, will bring an end to the ferocity, the rapine, and the crudities of Bolshevism surer than any other method.[8]

Nine days later, Lloyd George met in London with Nitti and new French Premier Alexandre Millerand, who had taken Clemenceau's place a few days before. Millerand proposed a policy of total isolation of Soviet Russia. Nitti declared that the moment had come to recognize Lenin's government. With Lloyd George acting as mediator (he may have set up the whole encounter together with Nitti), the three heads of state reached a compromise. They urged the nations that bordered on Russia not to carry out aggressive policies toward the Soviets. On the other hand, they declared that they did not want to open diplomatic relations with the Soviets until the "Bolshevik horrors" had ceased and Moscow had adopted "civilized" diplomatic behavior. They confirmed that the "economic blockade" was over and trade would be resumed.[9]

Clearly, the compromise was a success for Lloyd George's policy, as the conservative newspaper, the *Times*, pointed out in a critical commentary:

> It is impossible not to admire the profligate art with which for over a year Mr. Lloyd George had sought for his own purpose to throw a weak, ignorant, and reluctant Europe into the venal arms of her Bolshevist seducer.... The next step is to compromise her beyond recall. Then the path will have been opened for Lenin.[10]

End of the Economic Blockade

The anti-Soviet approach of both the British Conservatives and the French leaders made Lloyd George move cautiously. Between January and May 1920, the Prime Minister spoke as little as possible on Russian issues during his cabinet meetings. Those were crucial months and he preferred to act alone, so that not even his aides and colleagues were certain of exactly what foreign policy objectives he was pursuing.[11] On 15 March, speaking to the Commons, he continued to hide behind the shield of the cooperatives, claiming that dealing with them was not the equivalent of recognizing the Soviet regime. To save appearances, he added that he was not going to permit a politician like Litvinov to come to London to negotiate a resumption of trade.[12]

At the conference in San Remo, Italy, toward the end of April, Lloyd George again met with Nitti and Millerand. He repeated his intention to refuse to give Litvinov a visa for England or to establish diplomatic relations with Lenin's state. Thanks to these reassurances, he was able to take a decisive step in his policy of *rapprochement* with Moscow; he convinced France to authorize the opening of commercial negotiations with the Soviets. The meetings were to take place in London and the Soviet delegate would be Leonid Krasin.[13]

The Italian government joined Lloyd George in establishing contact with the Soviets. It sent socialist Member of Parliament Nicola Bombacci (a future founder of the Communist party) to Copenhagen to meet with Litvinov, authorizing him to negotiate both the question of Italian prisoners in Russia and the matter of resuming trade relations.[14] Another socialist parliamentarian, Angiolo Cabrini, who was a representative of the League of Cooperatives, was also sent to Copenhagen, and he signed a preliminary accord with Litvinov for the resumption of commercial exchange. Two more envoys, Virginio Gayda and Michail Kobilinsky, were dispatched to Denmark to meet with Litvinov. They reported that the Bolsheviks were "more concerned about reaching a political agreement with the Entente than resolving the trade issues."[15] Finally, Italian Prime Minister Nitti sent a diplomatic emissary, Giovanni Amadori Virgili, directly to Russia together with the former director of the Italian Institute of Moscow, Professor Odoardo Campa.[16]

Since the Italians were very well disposed toward Bolshevism, Krasin telegraphed Nitti requesting that they, rather than the British, host the trade negotiations between the Russian cooperatives and the Entente. The Soviets presumed the Italians would permit Litvinov to participate. Nitti was compelled to refuse Krasin's request, but he worded his reply very amiably:

I thank you for your telegram. It is in the interests of a general resumption of relations — which, more than just good business for Italy, I consider one of the ways to reconstruct European solidarity — it is in those very interests that I advise you, instead, to choose a neutral country. It would be fine if that country were Switzerland, which is nearest to us. I must add that, while it is my desire to establish excellent relations with Russia as soon as possible, I must also take into account certain inter-Allied considerations.[17]

Lenin could see the signs all around him that he had fortune on his side that spring. The speeches he gave in March and April of 1920 bear witness to this. "Soviet Russia proved to be the victor in a war against all the richest powers in the world," he proclaimed triumphantly. He attributed the victory to the solidarity toward Russia manifested by the Western proletariat. But he acknowledged that a decisive part was played by the mistakes made and paralysis displayed by the capitalist countries: "They were split owing to their wrangling, and their famous League of Nations turned out to resemble a league of mad dogs who are snatching each other's bones and cannot come to terms over a single question."[18]

17

The War between Russia and Poland

Relations between Soviet Russia and the West seemed headed toward gradual normalization, when suddenly in April 1920 the Russo-Polish war broke out. It was the Poles, not the Russians, who started it. Between 22 and 24 April, the Polish government signed a political-military accord with the head of the Ukrainian nationalists, Simon Petlyura. On 26 April, it announced that its army had invaded the Ukraine, and during the following days it overran the Red Army, conquering Kiev by 8 May. Though the Polish army did make initial gains, it was soon forced to pull back. In June and July came the Soviet counteroffensive, and by August the Polish troops had been pushed back to the outskirts of Warsaw. On 16 August, when the fall of the Polish capital seemed imminent, bringing with it the defeat of the Poles, Polish forces managed to turn the situation around, and not just temporarily. Pilsudski's army counterattacked and routed the Bolsheviks, so that by September they were requesting a cease-fire.

The repercussions of the war — not only in Russia and Poland but also in Germany, France, and Great Britain — created a complex situation, because the outcome of the war was uncertain and in each individual country the members of government held diverse allegiances. Historians usually affirm that Lenin, at the time of the conflict between Russia and Poland, believed anew in an impending revolution in Europe, thinking he could then export Bolshevism at bayonet point; but documents prove otherwise. To begin with, Lenin was well aware of all the anti-Russian feeling in Poland. He knew that a war would not change these sentiments; on the contrary, it would only reinforce them. He therefore had begun pushing for an agreement with Poland in 1919, through secret negotiations. In February 1920, the Polish Communist party adopted a prudent policy, in line with Lenin's cautious attitude. The Polish communists, in fact, proclaimed that the overturning of capitalism in their country could never occur at the hands of a foreign army, thus never by means of Russia's Red Army.[1] Lenin personally went out of his way to give the Poles further assurances in March 1920. He declared that he well understood the anti-Russian "hatred" that pervaded Poland. "We shall never cross the line on which our troops are now stationed," he stated.[2]

In May, Trotsky published "a warning against overly optimistic hopes of revolution in Poland" in the Soviet press.[3] The man who could be considered the greatest expert on Poland in the Comintern, Julian Markhlevsky, agreed with Lenin that the Russians should not deceive themselves.[4] Trotsky wrote in his memoirs: "We strained every effort to avoid that war."[5] During March and April, right up to the eve of the armed conflict, the Soviet government did try to prevent war from breaking out.[6] Nonetheless, Lenin insistently repeated his hopes for an outbreak of revolt in Poland, according to the testimony of Zetkin, Balabanova, Trotsky, and others. It is quite probable that he did hope for it, but with all the information in his possession, he could not have had many illusions about it. He knew that the Polish people's anti-Russian "hatred" was deeply rooted.

The war between the two countries broke out not because Russia wanted to export revolution, but rather because the Polish government was anxious to guarantee its own security permanently. From the close of the eighteenth century until 1918, Poland had remained partitioned among Austria, Russia, and Prussia. The defeat of the central powers and the chaos that ensued in Russia had permitted the Poles to regain their independence on 11 November 1918. But while the Versailles treaty gave the Polish state quite precise borders with Germany, the same could not be said of its borders with Russia, since the Soviet government was not represented at the Paris Peace Conference. The Poles, reminded of the former partition of their territory, intended to fix their eastern borders securely. Besides, the Poles were anxious to give Germany, Russia, and the rest of Europe a demonstration of the nation's strength. They wanted to affirm their hegemony over the Ukraine, perhaps even Lithuania, with the further goal of forming a sort of federation. All through 1919, the Polish government was concerned about the precarious condition of its boundaries and planned to put an end to this situation.

The Poles feared the re-creation of a Great Russia of any kind; but one governed by the Whites' generals, with the resulting support of the West, might have seemed even more threatening than a Bolshevik Russia. This was one of the reasons the Poles waited until April 1920 to make their move. They were hoping that the conflicting factions within Russia would wear each other down, and they also wanted to see which forces they would have to deal with in the future. By April 1920, the Poles realized that Lenin's men had beaten the Whites, that he was opening negotiations with the Entente powers (particularly with Great Britain), and that the Bolsheviks had supporters even in Germany, especially among the military. The danger existed, therefore, that the Polish state might find itself caught in a vise.[7]

Several documents might lead one to believe that Germany and Russia were preparing a repartition of Poland in 1920, similar to the one they eventually carried out in 1939. However, most sources do not support this hypothesis. Though both the Russians and the Germans were hostile toward Poland in 1920, the situation in Europe was quite different from that of 1939. In 1920, the Germans had recently suffered a military defeat. They possessed an army of only 100,000 men and were much weaker than the Entente. If they had collaborated with the Soviets in destroying the Polish state, they would have been invaded, in turn, by the French. It was better for Germany to wait out events and let the Soviets take the initiative. At that time, the aim of both countries was not the division of Poland, but more simply the revision of the Versailles treaty. If the Soviets succeeded in entering Warsaw and humiliating Poland, revision of the treaty would become necessary and inevitable. Then, the Germans could move to "defend" the former German regions of Poland and assure themselves a bargaining chip at the negotiating table. Lenin admitted that "by destroying the Polish army we are destroying the peace of Versailles, on which the whole present system of international relations rests."[8]

In Germany, naturally enough, political and military factions existed which opposed collaborating with the Bolsheviks, but in March 1920, these groups were in the minority.[9] General von Seeckt's position, instead, was very strong, and there was no doubt as to what his position was. He expressed it on 30 January 1920:

> As I consider the future political and economic understanding with Great Russia the immovable goal of our policy, we must at least try not to antagonize Russia. . . . I refuse to support Poland even in the face of the danger that she may be swallowed up. On the contrary, I count on that; and even if we cannot at the moment help Russia to re-establish her former imperial frontiers, we certainly should not hinder her.[10]

Three weeks later, von Seeckt gave a speech in Hamburg in which he reiterated his hostility toward Poland and his favorable attitude to Russia:

> To save Poland from Bolshevism — Poland, this mortal enemy of Germany, this creature and ally of France, this thief of German soil, this annihilator of German culture — for that not a single German arm should move. And should Poland go to the devil, we should help her go. Our

future lies in union with Russia, whether we like the present situation or not. No other road is open to us.[11]

The Bolsheviks, aware of the atmosphere in Germany, decided to sound out the terrain directly. In February 1920, two mysterious emissaries went to Berlin, and during meetings at the German Ministry of Foreign Affairs (perhaps with the Minister himself), they brought up the possibility of joint intervention in Poland. One of the envoys pointed out that this would put an end to the Treaty of Versailles and re-establish the old German border to the east. But the Germans replied that their participation in a war against Poland would be inadvisable, since it might persuade the Allies to invade Germany and divide it in two.[12]

It is often held that Lenin, after conquering Poland, intended to bring revolution to Germany. Documents show that the Berlin government firmly excluded such a possibility. On 16 February, Foreign Minister Müller told the committee on foreign affairs of the Reichstag that a Polish attack on Russia was likely, that the Russians would end up winning, and that their victory would facilitate Germany's re-acquisition of the eastern territories. Müller (who was to become Chancellor a few weeks later) emphatically rejected the possibility that the Soviets would either attack Germany or conduct revolutionary activity inside the Reich, because their desire to cooperate with Berlin was self-evident. All this was further confirmed by the fact that Berlin and Moscow were exchanging official representatives those very days, in the persons of Gustav Hilger and Viktor Kopp.[13]

With the friendly atmosphere prevailing between the two countries, General von Seeckt seemed tempted by the idea of splitting up Poland, while the Soviets continued probing the terrain in that direction.[14] In April 1920, Soviet representative Kopp asked to speak to the head of the Russian Division of the Berlin Ministry of Foreign Affairs, Baron Ago von Maltzan. At the meeting he repeated the proposal made two months earlier by the mysterious envoys previously mentioned. Kopp asked "if the opportunity existed to construct a combination between the army here and the Red Army for the purpose of a joint struggle against Poland." Von Maltzan clarified immediately that such a possibility did not exist.[15] The Soviet government found itself fighting alone against the Poles.

But there were other factors which made it possible to consider Germany a friend. On 7 July 1920, a newly signed accord between Moscow and Berlin elevated representatives Kopp and Hilger to the rank of consul, which gave them diplomatic immunity and use of codes and diplomatic couriers.[16] A few days later, at the foreign affairs ministry, Kopp proposed a full resumption of diplomatic relations and he announced that the Red Army was committed not to occupy the former German territories of Poland. This was a gesture that Germany could not leave unreciprocated. The following day, the Berlin government declared its "neutrality" in the Russo-Polish war, and prohibited any of the military aid that was being sent to Poland by the Entente from passing through Germany.[17]

During the summer of 1920, in political circles all over the world, it was suspected that secret Russo-German agreements existed to repartition Poland. The new German Minister of Foreign Affairs, Walter von Simons, felt compelled to furnish a denial in the Reichstag on 26 July 1920:

> Lloyd George has said that at this time there is a great temptation for Germany to throw herself into the arms of the Russians so as to evade the obligations of the Versailles treaty. We are not of this opinion. We do not want Germany to be turned into a battlefield between Eastern Bolshevism and Western imperialism.

Von Simons went on to praise Lenin's government for the order it had restored in Russia, and reminded his audience that Germany had recognized the Bolshevik government with the peace treaty of Brest-Litovsk in 1918: "We do not wish to treat the Russians as pariahs solely because we do not like their system of government. We ourselves have been treated as pariahs for too long, and we do not intend to adopt such an attitude against another country."[18] At about the same time, von Simons told the Italian ambassador that it would be impossible to restore the old regime in Russia, and that the Bolsheviks, who were advancing in Poland, did not in any way mean to threaten Germany, since they knew that, in such case, Germany would join with the Entente to defeat the Soviets.[19]

German public opinion, which was decidedly anti-Polish, generally agreed with the pro-Soviet stance of the government. In Berlin cafés the Russian advance through Poland was greeted enthusiastically.[20] The *Manchester Guardian*, on 23 July 1920, reported that German nationalists were increasingly ready to ally themselves with the Soviet state, which seemed to differ little from the czarist state in its basically military nature.[21]

Lenin was well aware of the deeply pro-Soviet sentiments widespread among German conservatives. In September 1920, he commented that in Germany, thanks to the advance of the Red Army on Polish territory, "an unnatural alliance of the Black Hundreds with the Bolsheviks" had been envisioned. (The Black Hundreds were reactionary bands that had raged through Russia after the 1905 revolution. They wanted the restoration of the old feudal society.) Lenin observed:

There has appeared a strange type of Black-Hundred revolutionary, like the backward rustic youth from East Prussia who, as I read in a German non-Bolshevik newspaper the other day, says that the Kaiser will have to return because there is no order, but one has to follow the Bolsheviks.[22]

In December 1920, Lenin proclaimed that "when the Russian troops were approaching Warsaw, all Germany was seething." He added that pro-Soviet behavior involved all classes of society: "The conditions of existence in Germany are compelling the German people as a whole, including the Black Hundreds and the capitalists, to seek relations with Soviet Russia."[23]

18
Lloyd George Receives Krasin at 10 Downing Street

During the Polish crisis, Lenin was encouraged by the Germans' attitude, but he was also reassured by the behavior of the Entente countries. They were unable to send troops to Poland and even had difficulty sending war *matériel*, since the German government, upon declaring neutrality, had precluded the use of its railway system. European dock workers, furthermore, refused to load arms onto ships headed for Poland. The manifestation of anti-Polish feelings in the West arose only partially from ideological reasons. It was caused mainly by the fear that the Russo-Polish conflict might spread and involve everyone. The First World War was barely over and people were weary of fighting. The Italian government, for instance, under the influence of a strong Socialist party, issued directives suspending all arms shipments to Poland.[1]

In spite of the friendliness demonstrated by France, the Poles found themselves in a dangerous state of political isolation, not only because of public opinion, but also because of the policies of the Entente powers, especially those of Lloyd George. In September 1919, the British Prime Minister had opposed the Polish proposal of going to war with the Bolsheviks.[2] In December, he commented to Clemenceau that the Poles had always been "a very troublesome people in Europe."[3] That month, not only Lloyd George, but also the entire Supreme Council of the Allies officially announced exactly what the eastern borders of Poland were to be — the so-called Curzon Line. This boundary would take the cities of Vilna, Brest-Litovsk, Leopoli, and Tarnopol away from Poland. The news naturally caused angry protests in Warsaw. In January 1920, Lloyd George advised the Polish Foreign Minister to come to some kind of agreement with the

Bolsheviks.[4] The following month, in the House of Commons, he publicly made it known that Great Britain would not support a Polish offensive against Russia.[5]

On 25 April, when the heads of state of Great Britain, France, and Italy were meeting in San Remo and were in the process of authorizing the opening of negotiations with the Bolshevik representative, Krasin, war broke out between Poland and Russia.[6] Clearly, the Poles were not only attacking the Bolsheviks but were also reacting to all the maneuvering against them carried out by the Entente powers, Germany, and Soviet Russia. However, Poland's initial success in the Ukraine did not make Lloyd George change his attitude. He was sure that the Polish army would be badly beaten.[7] The Prime Minister was doing a difficult political balancing-act, considering that there were several pro-Polish factions among the parliamentarians, the press, and his own cabinet ministers. He still intended to open negotiations with Lenin, and feared that the Russo-Polish war might endanger his plans. As he confided to Lord Riddell in May:

> There are two nations in Europe who have gone rather mad, the French and the Poles. Unless the Poles are careful they will revive and intensify the spirit of Russian nationality. Nothing can do this more effectively than arrogance on the part of foreigners. The Poles are inclined to be arrogant and they will have to take care that they don't get their heads punched.[8]

Polish aggression did not hamper Lenin's efforts to seek an accord with Britain any more than it prevented Lloyd George from aiming toward this goal. On 5 May 1920, three days before the Polish troops entered Kiev, Chicherin sent the British government another diplomatic note in which he repeated that "the earnest desire" of the Bolshevik government was still to reach "a general agreement with Great Britain."[9] A few days later, when the British telegraphed Moscow that they would be glad to receive Leonid Krasin, the invitation was enthusiastically accepted.[10] This was an historic turn of events. For the first time, a Bolshevik representative was to be officially received by government leaders of one of the Entente powers.

On 27 May, Leonid Krasin arrived in London heading a Bolshevik delegation. Four days later, he was received at 10 Downing Street by a welcoming committee that included Prime Minister Lloyd George, Secretary of the Foreign Office George N. Curzon, Lord of the Privy Seal Andrew Bonar Law, and Minister of Trade Sir Robert Horne. The chief Soviet representative, shaking hands with those present, extended his hand toward Curzon, but the Foreign Secretary made no move. Lloyd George then intervened saying: "Curzon! Be a gentleman!" At that point George Nathaniel Curzon, Baron Ravensdale of Ravensdale, Viscount Scarsdale of Scarsdale, Duke Curzon of Kedleston, found himself compelled to be courteous to the representative of those whom he considered responsible for terrible crimes, including the massacre of the Czar's whole family. Then the talks began.[11]

According to decisions made at the San Remo conference, the English were supposed to limit discussions to trade matters. But from the very first meeting, political problems were brought up. Krasin explained that the first condition for a resumption of trade was a formal end to the state of war. He pointed out that from the Soviets' point of view, the Entente was responsible for the aggression by the Poles. Lloyd George stated that Great Britain was not supplying any aid to Poland and had, indeed, advised the country not to attack. He then took up the subject he considered most important, declaring that it was time the Bolsheviks put an end to their subversive behavior in Asia: "Soviet emissaries were stirring up trouble in Asia Minor, in Persia, in Afghanistan, and among the tribes on the north-west frontier of India. Such actions must necessarily stop if trade was to be reopened on friendly terms." The British Prime Minister also asked the Soviets to put a stop to propaganda directed against any government of the Entente.[12]

Leonid Krasin met with the English again in the following week. This time Italian Chargé d'Affaires Gabriele Preziosi was present. Krasin declared that if peace were guaranteed, Russia would cease all anti-British activity everywhere, not only in the Orient, and that the same guarantees would be extended to Italy. Ex-Prime Minister Arthur J. Balfour asked the Bolshevik if Russia was willing to abstain from all propaganda in general. Krasin specified that "the government of the Russian republic was prepared to give an official undertaking, if an agreement were reached, not to carry on propaganda against the British empire. This undertaking would completely satisfy the wishes of the British government." Lloyd George asked, once again, if the other Allies could be included in this official commitment and Krasin answered affirmatively.[13]

It is no surprise that Krasin was ready to offer guarantees to the Allies and, particularly, to Italy. In Turin, some workers who were occupying the factories in September 1920 found an interesting document in the archives of the Fiat car company. It was a report sent from London, on 9 June, by a Fiat representative who had met with Krasin. The report stated that the Bolshevik envoy had shown considerable interest in purchasing Fiat trucks, had been very complimentary in his remarks about Italy, and had commented that within the Allied Supreme Council, Italy could be considered "the Left," while France represented "the Right" and England "the Center."[14]

Trotsky was one of the Bolshevik leaders who firmly believed that the talks taking place in London might lead to significant results. As he wrote Lenin, the British were split over the Russian issue and it might be advisable to restrain agitation in Asia in order to strengthen Britain's pro-Soviet factions. Lenin had decidedly different ideas on the matter, however. He was convinced that the British were being totally deceitful. "The talks between Lloyd George and Krasin have shown *with full clarity*," he wrote, "that England is helping and *will help* both the Poles and Wrangel. [Among the British] *there is absolutely only one line*."[15]

Lenin ordered the negotiations to continue, though, as he had his eyes fixed on the final goal, which was mainly political. He had no intention of throwing out his good cards in exchange for the mere resumption of trade. What he wanted was a general peace agreement and full recognition of the Soviet state by Great Britain and the other Allied powers. On 11 June, under Lenin's orders, Chicherin sent the following telegram to Krasin: "That scoundrel Lloyd George is fooling you in the most vile and shameful manner, don't believe a word, and fool him threefold."[16] Chicherin prefaced the telegram with more detailed instructions. It was not enough, he wrote, for Russia to be authorized to purchase such materials as, for instance, train locomotives, which they badly needed:

> However necessary locomotives may be we must not sacrifice everything for the doubtful possibility of perhaps getting a few of them. To show firmness does not imply the renouncing of results. You must in no way yield to British blackmailing. The situation that has been created in the East is a difficult one for England. In Persia they are almost helpless in the face of the revolution. Disloyalty is increasing amongst the Indian troops. . . . By a policy of capitulation we shall attain nothing . . . and if we do nothing else but make concessions, we shall not even get locomotives. The French demand for an embargo being placed on our gold is preparing the way for roguery on a large scale. You must believe absolutely nothing and show the greatest firmness.[17]

That same month Chicherin presented a long report on foreign policy to the Soviets' Central Executive Committee in which he emphasized the basic objective: "Our watchword has been and still is and will remain one and the same: peaceful coexistence with other nations, whatever types of government they may have." He placed much importance on Great Britain's foreign policy, which he considered complex, unpredictable and contradictory: "We will make an agreement with England, we are ready for it, but let it be a real agreement, binding on both sides, let there be genuine negotiations. We do not wish to be the victims of deceit." The commercial-financial "blockade" had to be completely dismantled and normal relations had to be restored:

> We want a political accord; we consider a trade agreement alone to be out of the question. But the accord must be bilateral, not binding only for us. . . . We are ready to give up total freedom of action so long as the other side, as well, abstains from hostile activities or attacks directed at us. That is our policy.[18]

The third meeting between Lloyd George and Krasin was held on 16 June. The Bolshevik representative, keeping to Moscow's line, made it clear that his government would abandon all forms of propaganda in Asia only if Great Britain accepted the idea of "a general peace." He cautioned that there were extremist factions in Russia which "preferred world revolution to world peace," although he added that these groups were in "a minority."[19] Lloyd George, too, was concerned about keeping his anti-Soviet "extremists" under control. On 17 June, in the House of Commons, the Prime Minister pointed out that it would be absurd not to trade with the Bolsheviks merely because they had a reprehensible government. Britain had always traded freely with lamentable governments: with the czar, not known for his liberalism; with the Turks, in spite of the atrocities they committed, and even with peoples known to practice cannibalism. One could, therefore, trade with the Bolsheviks.[20]

The discussions between Lloyd George and Krasin had taken on an obvious political nature, which, although more-or-less concealed from the Commons, could no longer be hidden from the French allies. On 20 June, Lloyd George met with French President Millerand and explained to him that the Bolshevik peril in Asia had compelled him to discuss political issues with Krasin. He specified that in Persia and Afghanistan, Britain had a contingent of 11,000 soldiers, and that the Soviets, by arming the local populations, would be able to cause these troops serious difficulties. Millerand, however, remained unconvinced. He disapproved of the way the London talks were evolving and he reiterated that the Soviet government was not to receive even de facto recognition.[21]

The situation became more complex when the probable outcome of the Russo-Polish war turned in Russia's favor. By 12 June, the Red Army had reconquered Kiev and sent the Polish troops fleeing. The Moscow government, which had already felt confident in facing the British over the Asian situation, began to feel even more bold after its military victories on the Western front. Chicherin telegraphed Krasin on 18 June to inform him that a part of the Soviets' Central Executive Committee (the "opposition," as it were) was urging the adoption of a more radical position in foreign policy: "All the appeals of the opposition speakers for adopting a more bellicose policy were met with rousing applause. This shows that a pacific and conciliatory policy is not very popular." The Foreign Commissar wrote that, since the masses were calling for resoluteness, it was "absolutely inadmissible to adopt before Lloyd George the tone of the accused."[22] A few days later, Chicherin succinctly stated the Soviet position regarding an accord when he wrote Krasin, "We must not sell it too cheap." According to Chicherin, they had to frighten the English with the threat of revolution in Asia:

> In unofficial conversations you must make it clear that we are able to cause them serious damage in the East if we so wish. Have them picture what would happen if we sent a Red Army to Persia, Mesopotamia and Afghanistan. We are awaited and yearned for there, and it is only the moderation of our policy which causes a slow development [of the revolutionary situation in those areas].[23]

Krasin expressed his fear that a coalition of nations might ally itself with Pilsudski and with Wrangel and then attack the Red Army. Chicherin reassured him:

> This is impossible. The feeling of the masses in the Baltic States precludes such an eventuality. Even the Finnish government shows striking evidence of its desire for peace. . . . Only a temporary cessation of negotiations is possible, but no active measures against us are. . . . Even Romania has shown no signs of wishing to join up with Poland even in the hour of the latter's victory, and now each day sees an improvement in our military situation.[24]

Finding himself ill at ease as a "trade" negotiator in meetings that had so evidently taken a political turn, Krasin asked Chicherin to join him in London.[25] But the Foreign Commissar refused:

> My coming to London now, when there are no formal peace negotiations, would be the greatest folly and humiliation. It would indicate that we are ready to agree to anything, and would completely ruin our policy of gradually extorting concessions from England, because she is too deeply committed, but she will continue as long as possible her two-faced policy, which we must meet by firmness.
> You must resolutely refuse any political promises as long as there are no real peace negotiations, and agreements about the East or in general about the cessation of a hostile policy must be left absolutely to the formal peace negotiations. . . .

It is necessary to repeat unceasingly and to emphasize in every possible way that we shall willingly agree to all such transactions, but shall agree only in the case of formal peace negotiations. Then, of course, we shall not permit any objection to our representatives and experts.[26]

Lloyd George, however, was not yet in a position to open such negotiations, because of French and English opposition, including some ministers in his own cabinet.[27] Furthermore, the *Times* on 11 June had printed a letter by Lenin to the English workers, whose harsh judgments on the British government and the ruling classes caused sharp reactions in public opinion. Lenin's letter was dated 30 May, the day before the opening of the London talks. In it he declared that the British government was obstinately rejecting the peace proposals and was sending arms to Poland. He announced that a communist party had to be set up to liberate the working class from ideological servitude to the bourgeoisie. He then went on to justify the Red terror and the measures adopted in Soviet Russia against freedom of the press:

Several members of your delegation questioned me with surprise about the Red terror, about the absence of freedom of the press in Russia, of freedom of assembly, about our persecution of the Mensheviks and pro-Menshevik workers, etc. My reply was that the real cause of the terror is the British imperialists and their "allies," who have been practising a White terror in Finland and in Hungary, in India and in Ireland, who have been supporting Yudenich, Kolchak, Denikin, Pilsudski and Wrangel. Our Red terror is a defence of the working class against the exploiters with whom the Socialist-Revolutionaries, the Mensheviks and an insignificant number of pro-Menshevik workers have sided.[28]

The purposely abrasive tone of the letter, written on the eve of the London talks, probably had a twofold aim: on the one hand, not to abandon the European Left just when the Bolshevik state was beginning to deal directly with the world's largest remaining empire; on the other hand, to spur the London government to open negotiations that had the purpose of "gradually wringing concessions" as well as "not selling cheap." In any case, Lenin's letter showed that Bolshevik diplomacy had taken on a new "style," concrete and traditional in its substance but disconcerting, even brutal, in its form. This was something Western statesmen were going to have trouble getting used to.[29]

The Lloyd George-Krasin talks reached a stalemate. At one last session on 29 June, Krasin reiterated that his government was ready to give up communist propaganda in Western countries in exchange for a trade agreement. It was not prepared, however, to abandon either its anti-West foreign policy or its anti-British activities in the Orient, including India, without a comprehensive peace agreement. Lloyd George replied that a resumption of trade was the necessary first step toward such a peace agreement and that, for this purpose, he considered an accord on ceasing hostilities to be essential. He added that what Krasin was saying to him "filled him with despair."[30]

Krasin requested a document summarizing the British position to take back to Moscow, and Lloyd George gave him a memorandum with which the Bolshevik representative left London on 1 July. In Point One of this document Lloyd George asked that Russia abstain from any form of military or propaganda activity, especially in Asia. This was the essential condition for any trade agreement. Such an agreement would then lead to the general peace accord that the Bolsheviks were calling for, but at a later date. This memorandum was important not only for what it said, but also for what it did not say. It did not contain any request for abstaining from hostile acts either toward Poland or toward the Crimea occupied by Wrangel. Lloyd George's proposals were concerned exclusively with Russo-British relations.[31] On 7 July, the Soviet government accepted these proposals, but only as a basis for broader negotiations that Russia intended to begin as soon as possible.[32]

19
Warsaw in Danger

By the beginning of July 1920, Poland's military position had become seriously jeopardized. Even though the Polish army was still fighting outside the country's borders, morale among the troops as well as the populace was waning. The war, started by the Poles to guarantee the nation's permanent security, was failing to achieve its goal.

The Polish situation was the center of attention at the Allied conference in Spa, Belgium, at the beginning of July. On 6 July, Lloyd George met with a Polish government official, Stanislaw Patek, to urge the Poles to begin negotiations with the Soviets immediately. He warned that otherwise the Allies would do nothing to help them. "Poland," he said, "would never get the active sympathy and support of Great Britain so long as she pursued an imperialist policy."[1] Several days later, Lloyd George made similar pronouncements to Polish Prime Minister Grabsky, who, already very demoralized, conceded that Poland was ready to change policy and abandon unrealistic ambitions.[2]

When Lloyd George met with Premier Millerand and Marshal Foch on 8 July, he asked Foch if France would be willing to send troops to Poland. The Marshal replied emphatically: "No. No men." Lloyd George then thought it opportune to explain frankly to the French Premier his reasons for negotiating with the Bolshevik Krasin:

> I said, "My object is peace." He [Millerand] seemed to my surprise to be rather pleased and said "oui-oui." I said the world wanted an end to all this bloodshed and conflict, and to settle down to business, and that our information was that these attacks upon Bolshevik Russia were simply strengthening not merely the communist government but the communist elements in the government, and that as soon as Russia was at peace, Russia would disintegrate.[3]

The French were still hesitant in aligning themselves with the British.

However, they did consent that the British write the Soviets a formal diplomatic note. The note, signed by Curzon and sent on 10 July, was a further step toward agreeing to Moscow's requests. It proposed: 1) an immediate armistice with the Poles, who would withdraw to the other side of the ethnic line established in 1919, 2) an armistice with General Wrangel, who would pull back inside the Crimea, and 3) a conference, to be held in London, between the Soviet state and the countries along its borders, that is, Poland, Lithuania, Latvia, Finland, and Eastern Galicia. Great Britain was volunteering to act as mediator for wide-ranging talks. Yet, these were not the negotiations opened to all the major powers, including Russia, which Lenin aspired to. The note asked the Soviets to answer within a week's time; otherwise, Great Britain would intervene militarily in defense of Poland — an empty threat, if there ever was one.[4]

Trotsky advised Lenin to accept the part of the British proposals involving Poland, but Lenin did not agree.[5] The current Polish military predicament seemed to offer the Russians much greater success. Lenin's decision was to reject the British ultimatum. He wrote his aides that Curzon's proposals were merely "a piece of knavery aimed at the annexation of the Crimea." He declared: "In my opinion [he] wants to grossly deceive us. He won't succeed." The Poles and the Entente were asking for a truce; it was essential not to concede one to them. "They want to tear victory out of our hands," he wrote Stalin on 13 July.[6] While rejecting the armistice, Lenin accelerated the offensive against Poland, realizing that it was vital not to give the Poles time to reorganize. On 12 July, Moscow signed a peace treaty with Lithuania, thus putting the Red Army in a position to march on Warsaw with its right flank protected. That same day, the Bolshevik chief wired his vice-commissar of war:

> Comrade Sklyansky, the international situation, particularly Curzon's proposal (annexation of the Crimea in exchange for a truce with Poland, the Grodno-Byelostok line), demand a *furious* acceleration of the offensive against Poland.[7]

Lenin believed that by defeating Poland (a logical follow-up to conquering Warsaw) and hence throwing into total disarray the decisions contained in the Versailles treaty, he would be able to compel the Allies to negotiate the general and definitive peace which remained his prime objective. The Bolshevik Central Committee confirmed his decision to turn down the British proposals.[8] Lenin wanted to stall for time (in order to march on Warsaw) but he did not want to burn his bridges with London. Thus, Chicherin's note in answer to Curzon did not close the doors on negotiating, and even offered the Poles more territory than the British had foreseen.[9] Lloyd George judged the Soviet reply to be most reasonable, and urged the Poles to request an immediate armistice with the Russians.[10]

The Poles asked for an armistice but the Russians were in no hurry to grant it, as the Red Army was still advancing toward Warsaw. Naturally, not all the Bolshevik leaders agreed it was wise to push this advance so far. Trotsky, for instance, spoke up against all-out war. Others maintained that it was foolhardy to expect the Polish people to rise up in favor of Russian Bolshevism. Still others were worried about the negative repercussions that the occupation of ex-German territories might provoke in Germany.[11] In particular, some Bolshevik leaders were at odds with Lenin because they felt that Germany, not Great Britain, was the nation to come to an understanding with. The Soviet representative in Berlin, Viktor Kopp, overstepped his mandate, however, when he offered the Germans a wide-ranging political accord. On 22 July, Lenin wrote Chicherin to admonish Kopp to deal with "only trade negotiations," and Chicherin telegraphed Kopp not to commit himself to anything political with the Germans.[12] The Bolshevik government had no intention of entering into accords that might seem to presage an alliance against the Western powers.[13]

Lenin saw the advantages of reaching an agreement with the British empire rather than the Weimar Republic. Germany was a recently defeated country with a small army, while the British empire had been on the winning side in the late war and was still powerful. A Russo-German political agreement could be used by Germany as a temporary instrument to wring concessions out of the Entente powers. The Soviet state instead, needed stable solutions which would allow it to reconstruct its economy after all the years of war and revolution. Furthermore, negotiations between the Bolsheviks and Lloyd George were already underway — and seemingly with bright prospects. To foster a favorable outcome to these meetings, German neutrality in the Polish war, coupled with the threat of a Berlin-Moscow alliance, would be better than an actual alliance, which might lead to unforeseen trouble.[14]

Meanwhile, the situation in Poland continued evolving in the Soviets' favor, and Lloyd George intended to take advantage of this to conclude an accord with Moscow. Having worked in vain for such an understanding since 1918–19, he now believed his goal was about to be accomplished. In 1918–19 the President of the United States had dominated the international scene; this time Lloyd George held center stage. Peace with Russia might mean an opportunity to revise the Versailles treaty, thus bestowing prestige on the "father" of this revision, Lloyd George.

As noted earlier, on 17 July the Soviets rejected the proposal to convene a "limited" conference in London. Three days later, Lloyd George responded that the British had made such a proposal because they thought it would constitute a link between Russia and the peace conference, thus smoothing the way for a better understanding between Russia and the outside world.[15] The Soviets felt they were within reach of their objective and did not intend to let it slip through their fingers. Chicherin's reply to the British Prime Minister on 23 July reiterated their final aim:

> The Russian government expresses its willingness to meet the desire of the British government as to its proposal to convene a conference with the purpose of establishing a definite agreement between Russia and other powers which participate in hostile actions against her or support such, and is of the opinion that the said conference ought to be composed of representatives of Russia and of the leading powers of the Entente.
>
> The Russian Soviet government agree that this conference should be called together in London. It makes known, at the same time, to the British government that orders have been given to the military command to meet the Polish *parlementaires* and to begin with *pourparlers* relative to armistice and peace.[16]

Lloyd George, satisfied with this answer, confided to Lord Riddell two days later: "This is a great occasion. The Russians wish the leading Allies to attend and, if necessary, the small nations whose territories abut on Russia, so that a general discussion on peace may take place. I am very pleased."[17] The Prime Minister lost no time; even before consulting with all the Allies, he sent Moscow a telegram saying the conference would be convened.[18]

Lloyd George met with the French Premier on 27 July, explaining that he had accepted the Soviet request because the news from Poland was "extremely bad." He added that the British cabinet had been unanimous in this decision and that even the anti-Bolshevik Winston Churchill had voted in favor of it. Now France's participation in the conference was indispensable. Italy and Japan had already received their invitations.[19] As expected, Millerand was very cross. He stated that a conference with the Soviets meant abandoning Poland. He was also worried about the increase in prestige that the Soviet government would derive from being placed on an equal footing with the great powers. He pointed out that such a precedent risked opening the way for a Russian-German agreement. Finally, he asked that, in any case, certain conditions be met by the Bolsheviks, among them a commitment to convoke a constituent assembly freely elected by the people.

Lloyd George replied that insisting on such a condition was tantamount to rejecting the conference. "The French," he commented dryly, "had been very good friends with the government of the late Czar, but they had never made it a condition of their friendship that the Czar should summon a constituent assembly." He maintained that delaying the conference would mean the collapse of Poland. In that case, Russia and Germany might well unite their forces against the Allies. He reminded Millerand, who did not even intend to grant the Soviets de facto recognition, that almost all the nations of the world, including France, had negotiated with the Bolsheviks on the repatriation of prisoners or on questions of trade, and thus had already given them de facto recognition.

Curzon, who was present at the encounter, acted as mediator. He suggested that in the first part of the conference the British, acting alone, discuss the Polish problem with the Soviets. Once that issue was settled, a second phase of the conference would begin with the French taking part as well. But French participation would remain subordinate to the Bolsheviks' acceptance of various conditions. According to Curzon, Millerand could rest assured that French adherence to the plan did not in any way entail de jure recognition of Soviet Russia.

Millerand finally capitulated, though he took pains to declare that it was "only out of deference to the British government and on account of his desire to help Poland, and it must be clearly understood that his acceptance did not in any degree involve the resumption by France of political relations with the Soviets."[20] Lloyd George understood that, though the French were still very hostile to recognizing the Bolshevik government, if a decisive event in the Russo-Polish war were to happen — such as the fall of Warsaw — it would not be difficult to convince them. The British Prime Minister was becoming impatient, however. He tried to reassure his friends that agreement with the Bolsheviks was worthwhile. When Lord Riddell expressed fear that Lenin and his comrades were trying to deceive the West, Lloyd George responded that the West's strong position lay in the fact that the Russians were probably in disaccord among themselves: Trotsky wanted war and "Krasin was not a Bolshevik at all."[21]

By the end of July, negotiator Krasin was on his way back to England from Moscow. This time he was in the company of a member of the Politburo, Lev Kamenev, who was now head of the Soviet delegation, while Krasin held second position. On 4 and 6 August, Kamenev and Krasin met with Lloyd George, but neither meeting led to any concrete results. Above all, the Soviets were interested in formal recognition for their state, not in the solution of the Polish problem. They had good reason to consider it more useful to leave the Polish question unresolved. Indeed, they could use

Russia's presence in Poland as a bargaining chip at any negotiating table with the Entente. Meanwhile, the Red Army was tightening its hold around Warsaw.[22]

Although Lloyd George felt no fondness for the Poles, he did not want to give the impression that they were being abandoned to their fate. Neither could he ignore that the French government put settlement of the Polish question before anything else. Therefore, it was necessary to impose a truce on the Russo-Polish conflict before a new peace conference of world powers could take place. The solution lay in a compromise that would satisfy the Soviets by leaving them many good "bargaining chips" and at the same time be acceptable to the Poles and the French. Lloyd George exhorted the Soviets to sign a truce "before" entering the Polish capital, and warned them that if Warsaw fell into the hands of the Red Army, the French would refuse to participate in the conference. He handed Kamenev a truce proposal which promised explicitly that the Allies would not use such a cease-fire to replenish Poland with men and supplies.[23]

On 8 and 9 August, the British Prime Minister talked with the French Premier, trying to convince Millerand to soften his intransigence. Lloyd George told him that defending Warsaw was not feasible, that there was the threat of the Russians and Germans uniting, and that Europe had not been in such peril since 1914. A Russo-German alliance, he added, would be "a most formidable [one]." As for the Poles, he still considered their behavior "foolish."[24] Millerand retorted that he was perfectly aware of the existing dangers, and he agreed it was impossible to send troops to Poland. His suggestion was to mobilize the Finns, the Rumanians, and the Estonians against Russia. He repeated that the West must not negotiate with the Bolsheviks because they were not trustworthy, and he claimed that French public opinion was behind him. Millerand went so far as to request the suspension of the talks with Kamenev and Krasin. But, to no avail.

Lloyd George countered that British public opinion differed radically from the French. In Great Britain the peasants were less than one-eighth of the population, the remainder being industrial. In France, on the other hand, half the population was made up of peasants. The two situations were clearly very different. The English Laborites and the trade unions would be able to mobilize public opinion against any involvement in the Russo-Polish war.[25] At the end of the second day of discussions, the two men signed a joint declaration containing only vague commitments in defense of Poland's independence.[26]

Aside from all the diplomatic documentation, further testimony of the British Prime Minister's efforts on behalf of an accord with Moscow can be found in several accounts by contemporaries. The Chief of Staff of the Army, Sir Henry Wilson, present at the discussion between Kamenev and Lloyd George on 6 August, made some significant annotations:

> I was horrified at the almost servile way in which Lloyd George looked after Russian interests and was hostile to the Poles. . . . The whole tone of Lloyd George shocked me very much. He was with friends in Kamenev and Krasin, and together they discussed the French and the Poles.[27]

It was during this 6 August meeting that Lloyd George presented the proposal for a Russian-Polish truce, but General Wilson deduced that the Prime Minister was not counting on such a truce at all. The General thought Lloyd George, Kamenev, and Krasin were stalling for time, awaiting the occupation of Warsaw by Soviet troops, which would break the stalemate in the talks:

> When I said that I thought we ought to write "from General Headquarters Russian Army and General Headquarters Polish Army" as very possibly the Poles would no longer be in Warsaw, the two Bolsheviks and Lloyd George burst out laughing, Kamenev having to stuff his handkerchief into his mouth. It was quite clear to me that all three knew, and that Lloyd George approved, of the occupation of Warsaw by the Bolsheviks.
>
> It was an amazing five hour meeting. It left me with a clear sense that Lloyd George is in the company of friends and kindred spirits when with the Bolsheviks. All through the meeting, the Bolsheviks, assisted by Lloyd George, were driving a wedge between the English and the French, and Lloyd George went so far as to say that if the French did not agree to the truce terms, then he would not support Poland nor make war on the Bolsheviks. WHEW![28]

Telegrams which the Russian delegates sent to Moscow confirmed that the talks were proceeding in a cordial atmosphere. Kamenev wired that the English were searching for a way out of the Polish question and were willing to concede to Soviet Russia "the most rigorous guarantees within reason, in spite of France."[29]

In Moscow, meanwhile, after lengthy discussions regarding the possibility of a truce, the Soviets formulated very harsh conditions for accepting one. A clause, in particular, provided for the establishment of a "Civic Militia," that is, an armed force under communist control, which would have had a decidedly negative effect on Poland's autonomy. On 10 August, Kamenev delivered a text to Lloyd George containing the conditions of armistice formulated in Moscow. He did not, however, include the part about the Polish "Civic Militia" — a clause he knew would have provoked sharp protest in England as well as France. On the basis of the document received, the British Prime Minister considered the Soviet proposals reasonable and urged the Poles to accept them.[30] Lenin exulted. He sent the following wire to Stalin the next day:

> We have just received a dispatch from the head of the Soviet delegation in London. Great Britain has flinched from a general strike, and Lloyd George has declared that he advises Poland to accept our armistice terms, including disarmament, the handing over of weapons to the workers, land distribution, etc. Our victory is a great one, and will be complete if we smash Wrangel.[31]

On the same day, he wired his emissary, Danishevsky, who was delegated to negotiate the armistice with the Poles, reminding him that Warsaw was to be considered a vital bargaining chip not to be given up:

> From Chicherin you will learn of our great diplomatic success in Britain in regard to Poland. I hope you will be fully able to take this into account and, in terms [of armistice], cleverly include Warsaw, as we agreed, along with the firmest guarantee of all the rest.[32]

Hence, the war the Red Army fought on Polish territory, often considered by historians to be tied to Bolshevik hopes of exporting revolution, was actually part of a diplomatic scheme, masterfully carried out by Lenin. As he said, the aim was to "ensure for Russia favorable terms of peace for many years."[33] Another purpose, of course, was to reduce Poland to the level of a harmless third-rate power, incapable of creating serious trouble in the future.

In several of his speeches in September–October 1920, Lenin indicated the probable outcome of capturing Warsaw. He pointed out that "the center of world imperialism's entire system, which rests on the Treaty of Versailles, lies somewhere very close to the Polish capital."[34] Occupying Warsaw meant ripping up the Versailles accord and establishing the conditions for a new international order which included the Soviet state, thus permitting it at long last to live and work in peace.

20

Russia in the International Community

The Russo-Polish war ended in an unexpected manner. On 16 August 1920, the Polish army counterattacked and defeated the Bolsheviks. The conference that was to be held in London among representatives of England, France, Soviet Russia, Italy, Japan, and the United States was, therefore, never convened.[1]

All the same, Lloyd George had no intention of suspending negotiations with the Soviets. He did not even want to break them off when serious improprieties committed by the Bolshevik delegation in London were revealed to the public. Chief Soviet delegate Kamenev had artfully omitted from the text of the peace proposals delivered to Lloyd George the clause pertaining to a Polish militia. This artifice, quickly discovered, caused some scandal. Kamenev had also got involved in British internal affairs by covertly financing (for the sum of £75,000) the Labor newspaper *Daily Herald*, as the paper itself reluctantly admitted on 10 September. In spite of these incidents, Lloyd George did not expel the head of the Soviet delegation; nor did he cut off the trade discussions with Krasin, which concluded with an Anglo-Soviet commercial accord on 16 March 1921.[2]

Lenin was aware that the defeat in Warsaw coupled with the Kamenev incidents would force him to shelve more ambitious political goals for a while. Yet, the outcome could be considered positive regarding Soviet Russia's relations with the rest of the world. The Entente powers were in no shape to make war on the Soviets; they were negotiating with them instead. The Whites' forces no longer posed a threat, and as for Poland, negotiations were underway for a peace treaty. Trotsky told American writer John Reed, on 24 September 1920, that Soviet Russia was preparing for peaceful coexistence: "Not only can we coexist with bourgeois governments, but we can cooperate with them within broad limits."[3]

In a speech Lenin made on 21 November 1920, he maintained that the successes of the Soviet government were "tremendous" considering the absence of any world revolution. Soviet Russia had entered the international community. In his view, the strongpoint of the Bolshevik state lay in its newly opened trade relations with the capitalist world:

> We achieved the main thing — the possibility has been maintained of the existence of proletarian rule and the Soviet republic even in the event of the world socialist revolution being delayed. In this respect it must be said that the republic's international position today provides the best and most precise confirmation of all our plans and all our policy. . . .
>
> Without having gained an international victory, which we consider the only sure victory, we are in a position of having won conditions enabling us to exist side by side with capitalist powers, who are now compelled to enter into trade relations with us. In the course of this struggle we have won the right to an independent existence. . . .
>
> If we cast a glance at the conditions in which we defeated all attempts made by the Russian counter-revolutionaries and achieved a formal peace with all the Western states, it will be clear that we have something more than a breathing-space; we have entered a new period, in which we have won the right to our fundamental international existence in the network of capitalist states. . . .
>
> The entry of the socialist country into trade relations with the capitalist countries is a most important factor ensuring our existence in such a complex and absolutely exceptional situation.[4]

With their victory over the Whites and with peaceful coexistence underway, the Soviets now had to devote all their efforts to the reconstruction of the Russian economy. "Communism," Lenin pronounced in the same speech, "is Soviet power plus the electrification of the whole country."[5] Only a greater productive capacity would enable the Soviet state to maintain its power and win the respect of the international community.

Lenin's aides had already been trying to persuade Western capitalists that communist Russia would be a more convenient partner than a Russia of the bourgeoisie. Former Trade Commissar Bronski expounded this theory quite openly in an interview published by the Italian socialist newspaper *Avanti!* on 5 August 1920:

> International capitalists know very well that a bourgeois Russia would be a financial weight on their shoulders; and this would mean new taxes; the obligations of a bourgeois state towards its own bourgeoisie would be enormous, and world capitalism would be compelled to take on these

obligations over the next two decades, while we are not a burden. A bourgeois Russian state would be unable to pay the foreign debts it contracted, while we can. We can pay not only with our gold but with our natural resources, our vast thick forests, our boundless and fertile soil, and our mines. If you are about to retort that even a bourgeois Russia could pay with these same means, I'll tell you right away, NO! Because the Russian proletarians would not work in a bourgeois state, while with us they work willingly without a timetable and without excessive salary demands, because they are directly involved in the régime that they themselves have created. I'll tell you something else: not only would Russian workers produce more but so would workers in other countries if they knew that their products were going to proletarian Russia. . . . The miners of Germany and Czechoslovakia have declared several times that if they knew they were working for [trade] with proletarian Russia they would refrain from striking and would increase their own working hours. That is the secret of our strength which a bourgeois Russia could not have.[6]

Ex-Commissar Bronski, in short, wanted it known that Soviet Russia and the capitalist countries would be able to set up a new and very original international organization of exploiters! Furthermore, Bronski's interview was printed in an Italian socialist newspaper while the Second Congress of the Communist International was meeting in Moscow. Historians usually say that the Second Congress represented the last revolutionary "wave" for the international communist movement before Lenin shelved his plans for world revolution, after the defeat in Poland. However, once Lenin was in power, those plans for global revolution were non-existent as far as he was concerned. He had wanted the Comintern to be founded for other purposes, in particular, to expand and tighten a network of communist parties that would guarantee the survival of the Soviet state. The Second Congress of the Comintern, held from 19 July to 7 August 1920, served those ends.

In its day, the Congress perplexed a good many people. They wondered at Lenin's motives. Why did he encourage the internal splits in workers' parties when the movement needed the broadest possible mandates in order to foster revolutionary uprisings? Why did he defend a "traitor-socialist" like Marcel Cachin, who had carried on pro-war propaganda during the First World War? And why did he so sharply attack Filippo Turati, who had been less inconsistent than Cachin? More generally, why did Lenin, who was usually pragmatic, seem so rigid and dogmatic regarding many issues involving the Comintern?

These questions can be easily answered in the light of the foreign policy conducted by Lenin and Chicherin from the start. Lenin did not fear the rifts within various communist parties because his aim was not world revolution. He may have feared, instead, being tied to communist parties that were broad-based, strong, and therefore largely autonomous. His long-range objective was to have parties which were faithful, disciplined, obedient, and prepared to go along with or to oppose bourgeois governments according to the shifting needs of Soviet foreign policy. He accepted Cachin and attacked Turati because the former recognized a need for total subordination to Moscow and the latter did not.[7] Lenin wanted discipline within the Comintern to be akin to the discipline he already maintained in the Bolshevik party. Strict limitations were imposed on parties seeking admittance to the organization, which was headquartered in Moscow. Furthermore, affiliated parties were not authorized to communicate directly with one another, but rather through Russia's party.[8]

An Italian delegate to the Second Congress of the Comintern, Giacinto Menotti Serrati, was one of the most rebellious against Lenin's directives. In particular, he opposed Lenin's ideas on the national and colonial issues. The Italian challenged the view that it was up to the communists to support the various liberation movements in Asia — be they democratic/bourgeois, nationalistic, or "chauvinist." Another delegate, Amadeo Bordiga, a future founder of the Italian Communist party, observed that Lenin's theories on the national and colonial questions revealed a sort of revisionism regarding the class struggle. Finally, the Indian representative, M.N. Roy, strongly condemned Lenin's views. But the Bolshevik leader prevailed over his opposition. The purity of party doctrine had to give way to "reasons of state."[9]

Lenin succeeded in fomenting divisions among European socialists when even the most shortsighted leftists could have seen that his aim was not to hasten revolution in their countries. In Italy, for instance, the Italian Communist party was founded in January 1921, when the idea of world revolution was already on the wane.[10] The defeat suffered by the Red Army outside Warsaw had destroyed many illusions, and the first Italian socialists who visited Soviet Russia had come back with reports of catastrophic living conditions among the Soviet masses.[11]

One might assume that in order to keep the Comintern's affiliates under tight rein and convince them to sacrifice their national interests, Lenin had to resort to questionable methods or make financial contributions to certain people and parties. These contributions existed, of course, but their importance should not be exaggerated. To keep the parties in line, the myth of the

Bolshevik revolution and its leader turned out to be extremely efficient. The communist movement's semi-religious ideology helped its members accept subordination and sacrifice.[12] From the beginning, the cult of Lenin was expressed in mystical terms. Already, in November 1919, the Italian socialist newspaper *Avanti!* had spoken of Lenin as a new messiah: "He has really led The Idea from heaven to earth, as Prometheus did with fire. For him The Word has become flesh, and is moving to conquer the world."[13] A year before, when ties had not yet been formed between Italy and Russia, *Avanti!* had made it clear to what extent the left wing of the Italian Socialist party was prepared to identify itself with the Bolshevik state:

> The Soviet republic is our country today. The proletariat finally has a homeland, and the working classes suffer when they see its glorious life in danger, and take heart in knowing it is secure and strong, and developing according to its free laws. To defend this land proletarians are willing to lay down their lives.[14]

Leninists were unquestionably ready to sacrifice the lives of their parties, the autonomy of their policies, and the independence of their ideas. In Italy and Germany, those renunciations contributed to the advent of the dictatorships of Mussolini and Hitler.[15]

Notes

LIST OF ABBREVIATIONS

ACS, Presidenza   Archivio Centrale dello Stato, Rome, Presidenza del Consiglio dei Ministri, Gabinetto, Serie speciale, Prima guerra mondiale.
ASMAE, AA.PP.   Archivio Storico del Ministero degli Affari Esteri, Rome, Archivio degli Affari Politici.
DBFP 1919–1939   E.L. Woodward and R. Butler, eds., *Documents on British Foreign Policy, 1919–1939*, First Series (London, 1947—).
DVP SSSR   Ministertsvo Inostrannykh Del SSSR, *Dokumenty Vneshnei Politiki SSSR* (Moscow, 1959—).
FRUS   United States of America, Department of State, *Papers Relating to the Foreign Relations of the United States* (Washington, D.C., 1931—).

CHAPTER 1

1. V.I. Lenin, "Our Revolution: Apropos of N. Sukhanov's Notes," *Collected Works*, vol. 33 (London, 1960), p. 480.
2. V.I. Lenin, "Moscow Party Workers Meeting: Reply to the Discussion of Report on the Attitude of the Proletariat to Petty-Bourgeois Democrats," *Collected Works*, vol. 28, p. 219.
3. Institut Leninizma pri TsK VKP (B.), *Protokoly Tsentral'nogo Komiteta RSDRP (B.): Avgust 1917 g- Fevral' 1918 g* (Moscow, 1929); Italian trans., *I Bolscevichi e la Rivoluzione d'Ottobre: Verbali delle Sedute del Comitato Centrale del Partito Operaio Socialdemocratico Russo (Bolscevico)* (Rome, 1962), p. 208.
4. Ibid., p. 194.
5. Ibid., pp. 209–211.
6. L. Trotsky, *The History of the Russian Revolution* (Ann Arbor, 1961), p. 167.
7. During the first half of November, signs of patriotic reawakening could be observed in the Italian population, including a good part of the working class, which until then had been indifferent or opposed to the war. Cf. P. Melograni, *Storia Politica della Grande Guerra, 1915–1918* (Bari, 1969), pp. 535–536.
8. P. Scheidemann, *The Making of New Germany: The Memoirs of Philipp Scheidemann*, vol. 2 (New York, 1929), p. 431.
9. L. de Robien, *Journal d'un Diplomate en Russie, 1917–1918* (Paris, 1967), p. 159.
10. See J. Bunyan and H.H. Fisher, eds., *The Bolshevik Revolution, 1917–1918: Documents and Materials* (Stanford, 1934), p. 240.
11. For the Brest-Litovsk negotiations, see R.K. Debo, *Revolution and Survival: The*

Foreign Policy of Soviet Russia, 1917–1918 (Toronto, 1979), pp. 21–169. For the social unrest that took place in Germany in January 1919, see P. Broué, *Révolution en Allemagne, 1917–1923* (Paris, 1971); Italian trans., *Rivoluzione in Germania, 1917–1923* (Turin, 1977), pp. 101–105.

12. V.I. Lenin, "On the History of the Question of the Unfortunate Peace," *Collected Works*, vol. 26, p. 445.
13. *I Bolscevichi e la Rivoluzione d'Ottobre*, p. 354.
14. Cf. I. Deutscher, *The Prophet Armed: Trotsky, 1879–1921* (London, 1954); Italian trans., *Il Profeta Armato: Trotsky, 1879–1921* (Milan, 1956), p. 325.
15. *I Bolscevichi e la Rivoluzione d'Ottobre*, p. 357. See also I. Deutscher, *Stalin: A Political Biography* (London, 1965); Italian trans., *Stalin: Una Biografia Politica* (Milan, 1969) p. 281.
16. *I Bolscevichi e la Rivoluzione d'Ottobre*, pp. 355–356.
17. See Debo, *Revolution and Survival*, pp. 126 ff.
18. *I Bolscevichi e la Rivoluzione d'Ottobre*, p. 353.
19. V.I. Lenin, "Seventh Congress of the R.C.P. (B.): Political Report of the Central Committee, March 7," *Collected Works*, vol. 27, pp. 98–99.
20. Ibid., p. 101.
21. Ibid., p. 102.

Chapter 2

1. Cf. L. Fischer, *The Life of Lenin* (New York, 1964), p. 110.
2. Z.A.B. Zeman and W.B. Scharlau, *The Merchant of Revolution: The Life of Alexander Israel Helphand (Parvus), 1867–1924* (London, 1965).
3. Deutscher, *Il Profeta Armato*, p. 144.
4. Parvus memorandum, May 1915, is published in Z.A.B. Zeman, ed., *Germany and the Revolution in Russia, 1915–1918: Documents from the Archives of the German Foreign Ministry* (London, 1958), pp. 140–152.
5. Cf. G. Procacci, ed., *La "Rivoluzione Permanente" e il Socialismo in un Paese Solo* (Rome, 1963), p. 156.
6. Zeman and Scharlau, *The Merchant of Revolution*, p. 158. For the relationship between Lenin and Parvus, see also A. Solzhenitsyn, *Lenin in Zurich* (New York, 1976).
7. In some texts Fuerstenberg's pseudonym, Hanecki, is written Ganetski or Hanetski, while Parvus' real surname, Helphand, is found as Ghelphand.
8. V.I. Lenin, "Telegram to J.S. Hanecki, 28 March 1917," *Collected Works*, vol. 36, p. 425.
9. Zeman, *Germany and the Revolution in Russia*, pp. 41 passim.
10. V.I. Lenin, "To J.S. Hanecki," *Collected Works*, vol. 35, p. 313.
11. V.I. Lenin, "Telegram to J. Hanecki," *Collected Works*, vol. 43, p. 624.
12. V.I. Lenin, "To Inessa Armand," *Collected Works*, vol. 43, p. 624.
13. See K. Radek's statement in F. Platten, *Die Reise Lenins durch Deutschland* (Berlin, 1924). The pamphlet is quoted in Zeman, *Germany and the Revolution in Russia*, p. 42.
14. V.I. Lenin, "To J.S. Hanecki and K. Radek," *Collected Works*, vol. 36, p. 444.

15. V.I. Lenin, "To J. Hanecki," *Collected Works*, vol. 43, p. 629.
16. V.I. Lenin, "To J.S. Hanecki and K. Radek," *Collected Works*, vol. 36, p. 445.
17. N.N. Suchanov, *Zapiski O Revoljutsii* (Berlin, St. Petersburg, and Moscow, 1923); Italian trans., *Cronache della Rivoluzione Russa*, vol. 2 (Rome, 1967), pp. 300–301.
18. V.I. Lenin, "Where Is State Power, Where is Counter-Revolution," *Collected Works*, vol. 25, p. 160.
19. V.I. Lenin, "An Answer," *Collected Works*, vol. 25, p. 220.
20. V.I. Lenin, "To the C.C. of the R.S.D.L.P. (B.): The Hanecki Affair," *Collected Works*, vol. 44, pp. 47–48.
21. V.I. Lenin, "Reference to J.S. Hanecki," *Collected Works*, vol. 45, p. 382.
22. See Zeman and Scharlau, *The Merchant of Revolution*, p. 165.
23. Zeman, *Germany and the Revolution in Russia*, p. 70.
24. Ibid., p. 94.
25. Ibid., p. 93. After the war, Diego von Bergen was in the service of the Weimar Republic as well as Hitler's Reich, becoming ambassador to the Holy See. Cf. Zeman and Scharlau, *The Merchant of Revolution*, p. 231.

Chapter 3

1. Much has been written about the relations between Bolshevik Russia and the Entente in 1917–18. During the most critical days of the Russo-German talks at Brest-Litovsk, some Bolsheviks were behaving in a friendly manner toward the Allied powers. On 1 March, for instance, when Allied troops landed at Murmansk, the Bolsheviks did not protest. Trotsky went so far as to wire the Soviet of Murmansk to accept the "aid" of the Allies. Cf. Debo, *Revolution and Survival*, p. 154. The Entente diplomats left Petrograd when the Bolsheviks signed the Brest peace treaty. But a few Western "representatives" maintained contact with the Soviet government. R.H. Bruce Lockhart, London's ex-consul general in Moscow, served this purpose for Great Britain; the United States made use of the head of the American Red Cross in Russia, Colonel Raymond Robins; the French left Captain Jacques Sadoul in Moscow, and the Italians General Giovanni Romei Longhena. Before they signed the separate peace at Brest, the Bolsheviks, in turn, had sent Maksim Litvinov to London and Lev B. Kamenev to Paris. Cf. R.K. Debo, "Litvinov and Kamenev, Ambassadors Extraordinary: The Problems of Soviet Representation Abroad," *Slavic Review* (September 1975): 463–482.
2. V.I. Lenin, "Decision of the C.C., R.C.P. (B.) on the International Situation, 6 May 1918," *Collected Works*, vol. 27, p. 355.
3. L. Trotsky, *My Life: An Attempt at an Autobiography* (New York, 1930). p. 389.
4. Fischer, *The Life of Lenin*, p. 273.
5. Zeman, *Germany and the Revolution in Russia*, pp. 93–94.
6. Ibid., pp. 94–95.
7. Ibid., p. 96.
8. Ibid., p. 107.
9. Ibid., p. 124.
10. Ibid., pp. 128–133.

11. G. Freund, *Unholy Alliance: Russian-German Relations from the Treaty of Brest-Litovsk to the Treaty of Berlin* (New York, 1957), p. 15.
12. Ministerium für Auswärtige Angelegenheiten der DDR, Ministerium für Auswärtige Angelegenheiten der UdSSR, *Deutsch-Sowjetische Beziehungen von der Verhandlungen in Brest-Litowsk bis zum Abschluss des Rapallovertrages*, vol. 1 (Berlin, 1968), pp. 629–633. See also Debo, *Revolution and Survival*, p. 221.
13. I.K. Kobliakov, "Bor'ba Sovetskogo Gosudarstva za Sokhranenie Mira s Germaniei v Period Deistviia Brestkogo Dogovora, Mai-Noiabr' 1918," *Istoriia SSSR* 4 (1958): 12. See also Debo, *Revolution and Survival*, p. 218.
14. V.I. Lenin, "Theses on the Present Political Situation," *Collected Works*, vol. 27, p. 362.
15. Cf. Debo, *Revolution and Survival*, p. 214.
16. Ibid., p. 220.
17. Ibid., p. 222. On the question of the Russian fleet in the Black Sea, see pp. 222–228.

Chapter 4

1. W.H. Chamberlin, *The Russian Revolution, 1917–1921* (New York, 1935), p. 2.
2. Commission of the Central Committee of the C.P.S.U.(B.), ed., *History of the Communist Party of the Soviet Union (Bolshevik): Short Course* (New York, 1939), p. 228.
3. V.I. Lenin, "Report on Combating the Famine, 4 June 1918," *Collected Works*, vol. 27, p. 431.
4. V.I. Lenin, "To A.A. Joffe," *Collected Works*, vol. 44, pp. 98–99.
5. See above, chapter 2. Lenin did not have complete faith in Ioffe either. At that time, Ioffe was expressing opposition to certain directives of both Lenin's and Chicherin's. He may have wanted Chicherin's position as Commissar. See V.I. Lenin, "To Ioffe and Menzhinsky, 24 May 1918,"*Collected Works*, vol. 44, pp. 90–92; "To Krasin, 3 July 1918," ibid., p. 113; and "To Ioffe, 3 August 1918," Ibid., p. 123. See also Debo, *Revolution and Survival*, pp. 309–311.
6. V.I. Lenin, "Telegram to J.V. Stalin, 30 June 1918," *Collected Works*, vol. 44, p. 111.
7. For the assassination of von Mirbach, see G. Leggett, *The Cheka: Lenin's Political Police* (Oxford, 1981), pp. 70–83; Debo, *Revolution and Survival*, p. 316; G. Hilger and A.G. Meyer, *The Incompatible Allies: A Memorial-History of German-Soviet Relations, 1918–1941* (New York, 1953), pp. 2 ff. The assassination took place in the building that was to become the Italian Embassy, and for many years a stain of Count Mirbach's blood remained on the parquet floor, covered by a rug.
8. Lersner (High Command) to Foreign Ministry (Berlin), telegram, 11 July 1918, Verhältnis Deutschlands zu Russland, n. 84, St. Antony's College, Oxford; quoted in Freund, *Unholy Alliance*, p. 22.
9. Cf. Debo, *Revolution and Survival*, pp. 328–331.
10. Ibid., pp. 339–341. See also Fischer, *The Life of Lenin*, p. 268.
11. Debo, *Revolution and Survival*, p. 342. The German ambassador's anti-sovietism is confirmed in his book of memoirs. See K.T. Helfferich, *Der Weltkrieg* (Karlsruhe, 1925), pp. 639 ff.

12. Debo, *Revolution and Survival*, p. 343. See also W. Baumgart, *Deutsche Ostpolitik, 1918* (Vienna and Munich, 1966) pp. 392-394.
13. Debo, *Revolution and Survival*, pp. 348–350 and p. 390; and Freund, *Unholy Alliance*, p. 29. Fundamental sources of material on the Russian-German negotiations are the documents published by the Foreign Ministries of both nations in 1967–1971 (see above chapter 3, note 12). The secret agreement of 27 August is also published in J. Degras, ed., *Soviet Documents on Foreign Policy*, vol. 1 (London, 1951), pp. 96–98.
14. L. Fischer, *The Soviets in World Affairs: A History of the Relations between the Soviet Union and the Rest of the World, 1917–1929*, vol. 1 (Princeton, N.J., 1951), pp. 130–131. According to Freund, *Unholy Alliance*, p. 29, the 27 August accords, except for the clauses pertinent to the indemnities, were "totally different from the unilateral peace treaty signed in Brest six months earlier."
15. M. Philips Price, *My Reminiscences of the Russian Revolution* (London, 1921), p. 343.
16. G. Chicherin, *Stat'i i Rechi po Voprosam Mezhdunarodnoi Politiki* (Moscow, 1961), p. 66. Chicherin is also quoted in Debo, *Revolution and Survival*, p. 353.
17. Radek's speech, given on 3 September, was published in *Izvestiia*, 6 September 1918. Cf. A.L.P. Dennis, *The Foreign Policies of Soviet Russia* (New York, 1924), pp. 45–46.
18. V.I. Lenin, "Speech at a Joint Session of the All-Russia Central Executive Committee, the Moscow Soviet, Factory Committees and Trade Unions of Moscow, 29 July 1918," *Collected Works*, vol. 28, p. 29.
19. A great deal of information on this matter is contained in Fischer, *The Life of Lenin*, pp. 280 ff. For Fanja (or Dora) Kaplan, whose real last name was Roidman, see also Leggett, *The Cheka*, pp. 106–108.

CHAPTER 5

1. Cf. the speech Lenin made on 7 March, already cited in chapter 1, notes 19–21.
2. For Litvinov's declaration, see L. Fischer, *Men and Politics: An Autobiography* (New York, 1941), p. 127.
3. K. Radek, "November," *Krasnaya Nov* (October 1926); rpt. in E.H. Carr, "Radek's 'Political Salon' in Berlin, 1919," *Soviet Studies* 3 (1952), pp. 415–418. Lenin feared the Germans might join the Entente countries to fight against Soviet Russia.
4. Philips Price, *My Reminiscences of the Russian Revolution*, p. 345.
5. DVP SSSR, vol.1, pp. 557-558.
6. The fact that the embassy personnel totalled 186 people is found in Debo, *Revolution and Survival*, p. 396. The expulsion of Ioffe was a sign of the new turn taken by Berlin in foreign affairs after the Allied victory. The German government may have been annoyed and perhaps frightened by the more-or-less clandestine propaganda activity that Ioffe and the other Soviet diplomats residing in Berlin were carrying on. But the importance of these activities should not be overestimated. Ioffe personally confessed to Louis Fischer that he had done little or nothing to provoke revolution in Germany. "We were too weak," he told him. See Fischer, *Men and Politics*, p. 26. The Germans expelled Ioffe because they found propaganda material in a box addressed to him. Actually, the material had

been put there by German agents who then saw to it that when the box reached the Berlin station it dropped, broke open, and revealed its contents. Chicherin spoke of this episode as a "vaudeville incident" in which "leaflets that we had never put in the box" were found. See G. Chicherin, *Two Years of Soviet Foreign Policy* (New York, 1920), p. 24. For this incident, see DVP SSSR, vol.1, p. 560; Scheidemann, *The Making of New Germany*, vol. 2, pp. 532–535; and M. Fainsod, *International Socialism and the World War* (New York, 1966), pp. 177–179. Ioffe was on his way back to Moscow when he received news of the Kaiser's fall from power. He interrupted his trip home, hoping vainly that the new German Social Democratic government would permit him to return to Berlin.
7. Cf. K. Radek, "November," in E.H. Carr, "Radek's 'Political Salon,'" pp. 416–417. See also DVP SSSR, vol. 1, pp. 570–571.
8. Philips Price, *My Reminiscences of the Russian Revolution*, pp. 350–351; and A. Ascher, "Russian Marxism and the German Revolution, 1917–1920," in *Archiv für Sozialgeschichte*, vol. 6–7 (Hannover, 1967), p. 408.
9. V.I. Lenin, "'Democracy' and Dictatorship," *Collected Works*, vol. 28, p. 372. The article, dated 23 December 1918, was published in *Pravda*, 3 January 1919.
10. Broué, *Rivoluzione in Germania, 1917–1923*, p. 205.
11. Ibid., pp. 131, 147 and 176–177.
12. R. Luxemburg's article was published in *Die Neue Zeit*, 13 and 20 July 1904; Italian trans., "Problemi di Organizzazione della Socialdemocrazia Russa," in *Scritti Politici*, ed. L. Basso (Rome, 1967), p. 226.
13. *Scritti Politici*, p. 232.
14. V.I. Lenin, "One Step Forward, Two Steps Back: Reply by Lenin to Rosa Luxemburg," *Collected Works*, vol. 7, pp. 475 and 482.
15. R. Luxemburg is quoted in B. Lazitch and M.M. Drachkovitch, *Lenin and the Comintern*, vol. 1 (Stanford, 1972), p. 68.
16. Ibid., pp. 66–67.
17. V.I. Lenin, "The Right of Nations to Self-Determination," *Collected Works*, vol. 20, pp. 404–405.
18. V.I. Lenin, "To Inessa Armand," *Collected Works*, vol. 43, pp. 417–420.
19. R. Luxemburg, "Die Russische Tragödie," *Spartacus* 11 (September 1918); Italian trans., *Scritti Scelti*, ed. L. Amodio (Turin, 1975), pp. 548 and 551–552.
20. I. Martov, "Ein Brief an die Deutschen Genossen," *Der Sozialist* 4 (1918): 12; rpt. in A. Ascher, *The Mensheviks in the Russian Revolution* (Ithaca, N.Y., 1976), pp. 117–118.
21. K. Radek, "November," in Carr, "Radek's 'Political Salon,'" p. 418.
22. Cf. Broué, *Rivoluzione in Germania, 1917–1923*, pp. 39–40.
23. V.I. Lenin, "Rosa Luxemburg and the Polish 'Partei' Vorstand in Martov's Wake," *Collected Works*, vol. 41, pp. 255–260.
24. R. Fischer, *Stalin and German Communism* (Cambridge, Mass., 1948), p. 76.
25. Between 5 and 9 January 1919, a few Spartacists, including Karl Liebknecht, had illusions that they could overthrow the government by revolutionary insurrection. But Radek opposed the undertaking and found that Luxemburg was basically in agreement with him. See Broué, *Rivoluzione in Germania, 1917–1923*, pp. 233–240.
26. Cf. Fischer, *Stalin and German Communism*, p. 76.
27. Cf. Luxemburg, "La Rivoluzione Russa," in *Scritti Politici*, pp. 553–595.

Notes to Pages 34–39   131

28. Ibid., pp. 590–591.
29. Broué, *Rivoluzione in Germania, 1917–1923*, p. 205.
30. Ibid., pp. 205–206. Luxemburg's proposal was defeated because the heads of the League were split on the matter: three members voted for it, four against it.
31. H. Eberlein, "Die Gründung der Komintern und der Spartakusbund," *Die Kommunistische Internationale*, 13 March 1929, pp. 676–677; rpt. in Lazitch and Drachkovitch, *Lenin and the Comintern*, p. 61.
32. Broué, *Rivoluzione in Germania, 1917–1923*, pp. 234 and 237; and Lazitch and Drachkovitch, *Lenin and the Comintern*, pp. 98–99.
33. Luxemburg wrote that the workers had taken up arms in order "not to weaken... the moral standing of the German revolution in the International." See Broué, *Rivoluzione in Germania, 1917–1923*, p. 240.
34. Ibid., p. 242.

Chapter 6

1. V.I. Lenin, "Extraordinary Seventh Congress of the R.C.P. (B.), 6–8 March 1918," *Collected Works*, vol. 27, p. 106.
2. V.I. Lenin, "The Chief Task of Our Day," ibid., p. 163; and "The Immediate Tasks of the Soviet Government," ibid., p. 259.
3. V.I. Lenin, "On the Famine: A Letter to the Workers of Petrograd," ibid., 396.
4. V.I. Lenin, "Original Version of the Article 'The Immediate Tasks of the Soviet Government': Verbatim Report," ibid., p. 203.
5. Ibid., p. 204.
6. V.I. Lenin, "The Character of Our Newspapers," *Collected Works*, vol. 28, pp. 96–97.
7. V.I. Lenin, "Six Theses on the Immediate Tasks of the Soviet Government," *Collected Works*, vol. 27, p. 316. The article was written between 30 April and 3 May 1918.
8. Ibid.
9. V.I. Lenin, "Report on the Activities of the Council of People's Commissars, 11 (24) January 1918," *Collected Works*, vol. 26, p. 456.
10. V.I. Lenin, "Original Version of the Article 'The Immediate Tasks of the Soviet Government,'" *Collected Works*, vol. 27; p. 213. For the end of "workers' control" and the protests of the Petrograd workers, see M. Geller and A. Nekric, *Storia dell' URSS dal 1917 a Oggi: L'Utopia al Potere* (Milano, 1984), pp. 58–60.
11. V.I. Lenin, "Reply to the Debate on the Report on Ratification of the Peace Treaty," *Collected Works*, vol. 27, p. 195.
12. V.I. Lenin, "The State and Revolution" (chapter 5, n. 4), *Collected Works*, vol. 25, p. 478.
13. V.I. Lenin, "Moscow Party Workers Meeting: Reply to the Discussion of Report on the Attitude of the Proletariat to Petty-Bourgeois Democrats," *Collected Works*, vol. 28, p. 219.
14. V.I. Lenin, "Report on the Party Program, 19 March 1919," *Collected Works*, vol. 29, p. 179.
15. V.I. Lenin, "Report on the Role and Tasks of the Trade Unions, 23 January 1921," *Collected Works*, vol. 32, p. 61.

16. P. Melograni, *Fascismo, Comunismo e Rivoluzione Industriale* (Rome-Bari, 1984), pp. 65 ff.
17. V.I. Lenin, "Speech at a Joint Meeting of the Petrograd Soviet of Workers, and Soldiers' Deputies and Delegates from the Fronts" *Collected Works*, vol. 26, p. 294.
18. Rosa Luxemburg herself gave voice to this approach when she wrote, "The proletarian revolution has no need for terror." See "La Rivoluzione Russa," in *Scritti Politici*, p. 582.
19. V.I. Lenin, "Decree on the Arrest of the Leaders of the Civil War against the Revolution," *Collected Works*, vol. 26, p. 351; and "Meeting of the All-Russia Central Executive Committee, 1 (14) December 1917," ibid., p. 354.
20. V.I. Lenin, "How to Organize Competition?", *Collected Works*, vol. 26, p. 414. For the executions without trial, see also "Meeting of Presidium of the Petrograd Soviet with Delegates from Food Supply Organizations, 14 (27) January 1918: On Combating the Famine," ibid., pp. 501–502; "The Socialist Fatherland Is in Danger!", *Collected Works*, vol. 27, pp. 30–33; and "The Chief Task of Our Day," ibid., pp. 159–163.
21. Cf. J. Bunyan and H.H. Fisher, eds., *The Bolshevik Revolution, 1917–1918*, pp. 580–581.
22. J.V. Stalin, "Telegram to Sverdlov, Chairman of the All-Russian Central Executive Committee, 31 August 1918," *Works*, vol. 4 (Moscow, 1953), p. 130.
23. E.H. Carr, *The Bolshevik Revolution, 1917–1923*, vol. 1 (London, 1950), p. 168.

Chapter 7

1. V.I. Lenin, "To L. Kamenev," *Collected Works*, vol. 44, p. 149.
2. V.I. Lenin, "The Proletarian Revolution and the Renegade Kautsky," *Collected Works*, vol. 28, p. 113.
3. Quoted in I. Gorokhov, L. Zamiatin and I. Zemskov, *G.V. Chicherin: Diplomat Leninskoi Skholy* (Moscow, 1966), pp. 47–78. Cf. Debo, *Revolution and Survival*, p. 385.
4. V.I. Lenin, "To G.V. Chicherin and L.M. Karakhan," *Collected Works*, vol. 44, p. 152.
5. Fischer, *The Soviets in World Affairs*, p. 150. The complete text of Chicherin's diplomatic note is rpt. in Degras, *Soviet Documents on Foreign Policy*, vol. 1, pp. 112–120. For the dismay caused in the West by the "unusual" style of the note, see *Le Temps*, 23 January 1919, p. 1.
6. All the Soviet initiatives taken in November–December 1918 are listed in a message by Chicherin, 12 January 1919, rpt. in DVP SSSR, vol. 2, pp. 24–26. For an English translation of the document, see FRUS, *1919, Russia*, pp. 8–9. The 3 November request for an armistice is in DVP SSSR, vol. 2, p. 549.
7. DVP SSSR, vol. 1, pp. 628–630. An English translation of the document is published in C.K. Cumming and W.W. Pettit, eds., *Russian American Relations, March 1917–March 1920: Documents and Papers* (New York, 1920), pp. 270–273.
8. Cf. Degras, *Soviet Documents on Foreign Policy*, vol. 1, pp. 133–135.
9. See above, note 6.
10. P. Rowland, *Lloyd George* (London, 1975), pp. 497–498.

11. FRUS, *The Paris Peace Conference, 1919*, vol. 3, pp. 643–646.
12. FRUS, *1919, Russia*, pp. 10–14 and 19–22. These are the minutes of the meetings held in Paris, 16 and 21 January 1919.
13. For the extent of the Allied military intervention in Russia, see G. Boffa, *Storia dell'Unione Sovietica*, vol. 1 (Milan, 1976), pp. 120–121. According to Boffa, "the number of English, American, French and Italian troops was rather small, inadequate to any plan of action on a vast scale and considerably lower than the figures that the White Army generals and other anti-Bolshevik forces had been led to believe." Most Allied intervention was carried out indirectly, in the form of aid to the White forces. Cf. Geller and Nekric, *Storia dell'URSS dal 1917 a Oggi*, pp. 96–99.

CHAPTER 8

1. For the invitation to the Prinkipo meeting, see FRUS, *1919, Russia*, pp. 30–31. The invitation was a result of a compromise. Cf. "Editorial," *Le Temps*, 24 January 1919. See also Lloyd George's speech to the House of Commons, Session of 12 February 1919, published in *The Parliamentary Debates: Official Report*, Fifth Series, vol. 112, pp. 193 ff. Lloyd George said that there had never been a proposal to recognize the Bolsheviks. It had never been suggested, moreover, that they took part in the peace conference.
2. W.P. and Z.K. Coates, *A History of Anglo-Soviet Relations*, with a preface by D. Lloyd George (London, 1943), p. xiii.
3. On this matter, see *Le Temps*, 4 and 5 February 1919; and Fisher, *The Life of Lenin*, p. 348.
4. Frazier Hunt's correspondence was published in the Italian newspaper *Avanti!* (Piedmont edition), 19 May 1919, p. 2.
5. V.I. Lenin, "Telegram to L.D. Trotsky, 24 January 1919,"*Collected Works*, vol. 44, p. 191.
6. The document is rpt. in Degras, *Soviet Documents on Foreign Policy*, vol. 1, pp. 137–139.
7. *Avanti!*, 9 February 1919, p. 1.
8. The delegates named by the governments of the Entente were: G.D. Herron and M.W.A. White (for the United States), M. Borden (Canadian Prime Minister, for the British Commonwealth), M. Conty (Minister to Copenhagen, for France), P. Tomasi della Torretta (ex-ambassador to Petrograd, for Italy). Cf. *Le Temps*, 9 February 1919, p. 1.
9. In 1933, Bullitt was named ambassador to Moscow by President Roosevelt. In 1919, Bullitt had left for Moscow accompanied by the writer Lincoln Steffens — known for his pro-Bolshevik views — and by Captain Walter W. Pettit of the Military Intelligence Corps. (Later, Pettit edited the collection of documents on American-Russian relations mentioned above in Chapter 7, note 7). For Bullitt's mission, see B. Farnsworth, *William Bullitt and the Soviet Union* (Bloomington, Ind., 1967). For Lincoln Steffens, cf. J. Kaplan, *Lincoln Steffens: A Biography* (New York, 1974). See also P.G. Filene, *Americans and the Soviet Experiment, 1917–1933* (Cambridge, Mass., 1967).
10. This extraordinary Soviet offer was so totally forgotten that when a historian

found reference to it in the archives in 1981, the Associated Press sent it over teletype as a news item. Cf. "Historian Says Lenin Offered Bulk of Russia for Recognition," *Daily American*, 22 April 1981, p. 3.
11. FRUS, *1919, Russia*, pp. 77–80.
12. Ibid., p. 87.
13. Dennis, *The Foreign Policies of Soviet Russia*, p. 78.
14. Years later, Rakovsky showed Louis Fischer the letters Chicherin had written him. Cf. Fischer, *Men and Politics*, pp. 132–133.
15. V.I. Lenin, "Report on the Foreign and Home Policy of the Council of People's Commissars," *Collected Works*, vol. 29, pp. 19–25; and "The Achievements and Difficulties of the Soviet Government," ibid., pp. 57–63.
16. W.C. Bullitt, *The Bullitt Mission to Russia: Testimony before the Committee on Foreign Relations, United States Senate* (Westport, Ct., 1977), pp. 65–66 and 73. See also H.W. Steed, *Through Thirty Years* (London, 1924); Italian trans., *Trent' Anni di Storia Europea, 1892–1922* (Milan, 1962), pp. 559–561. On 18 March, L. Martens presented his credentials as the representative of Soviet Russia to the United States, but he was refused recognition. Cf. FRUS, *1919, Russia*, pp. 133–141.
17. *Le Temps*, 22 April 1919.
18. V.I. Lenin, "To G.V. Chicherin — M.M. Litvinov," *Collected Works*, vol. 44, pp. 224–226.
19. I. Don Levine, *Eyewitness to History: Memoirs and Reflection of a Foreign Correspondent for Half a Century* (New York, 1973), pp. 65–68.
20. V.I. Lenin, "Answers to an American Journalist's Questions," *Collected Works*, vol. 29, p. 517.
21. V.I. Lenin, "Answers to Questions Put by a *Chicago Daily News* Correspondent, 5 October 1919," *Collected Works*, vol. 30, pp. 50–51. The interview was given to Levine in writing and it was published in the *Chicago Daily News*, 27 October 1919. See Levine, *Eyewitness to History*, p. 79.
22. *The Parliamentary Debates: Official Report*, Fifth Series, vol. 120, pp. 1576–1577. Besides receiving Malone, Chicherin talked with I.D. Levine, to whom he repeated: "Our position regarding peace has not changed since March, when the Bullitt mission arrived here. . . . We are ready at any time to negotiate peace, provided recognition be given to all the existing governments in the territory of the former Russian empire, the Allied blockade be raised, mutual amnesties be given, and there be a simultaneous demobilization of all armies operating within the limits of the former Russian empire. We are willing to assume the national debt of the empire." See Levine, *Eyewitness to History*, p. 78.
23. Boffa, *Storia dell'Unione Sovietica*, vol. 1, p. 109.
24. Levine's report was published originally in the *Chicago Daily News*, 30 May 1919, rpt. in *Eyewitness to History*, p. 66.

Chapter 9

1. Bullitt's memorandum is in FRUS, *1919, Russia*, p. 92.
2. Cf. Lazitch and Drachkovitch, *Lenin and the Comintern*, pp. 54, 58 and 67–75; and H. Guilbeaux, *Du Kremlin au Cherche-Midi* (Paris, 1933), pp. 214–215. The

Italian Socialist party was not represented at the assembly. However, in order to give a semblance of greater authority to the congress, Lenin asked Angelica Balabanova to announce that party's support. Balabanova refused, since she had not received any specific mandate from the Italians. She wrote: "Lenin resented my refusal.... 'But you read *Avanti!* and are well informed,' he replied in writing. I repeated my refusal." See A. Balabanoff, *La mia Vita di Rivoluzionaria* (Milan, 1979), p. 175.
3. Lazitch and Drachkovitch, *Lenin and the Comintern*, pp. 50 ff.
4. See above, chapter 5, note 30.
5. H. Eberlein, "Die Gruendung der Komintern und der Spartakusbund," *Die Kommunistische Internationale*, 13 March 1929, pp. 666–667.
6. A. Balabanoff, *Ricordi di una Socialista* (Rome, 1946), p. 210.
7. The motion is reprinted in A. Agosti, ed., *La Terza Internazionale: Storia Documentaria*, vol. 1 (Rome, 1974), p. 42.
8. Ibid., p. 21.
9. V.I. Lenin, "The Third International and its Place in History," *Collected Works*, vol. 29, p. 310.
10. Balabanoff, *Lenin Visto da Vicino* (Rome, 1959), p. 91.
11. Agosti, *La Terza Internazionale*, p. 80.
12. Ibid., p. 81.

Chapter 10

1. At the founding congress of the Comintern, the Hungarian communists were represented by E. Rudnyansky, an ex-prisoner of war who had remained in Russia and was not in contact with his comrades in Budapest. See Lazitch and Drachkovitch, *Lenin and the Comintern*, pp. 68 and 135.
2. L. Valiani, "La Politica Estera dei Governi Rivoluzionari Ungheresi del 1918–1919," *Rivista Storica Italiana* (December 1966): 890.
3. Ibid., pp. 890–891.
4. Ibid., pp. 894–895.
5. Bullitt, *The Bullitt Mission to Russia*, p. 66.
6. Ian C. Smuts, "To A. Clark," in W.K. Hancok and J. van der Poel, eds., *Selections from the Smuts Papers, November 1918–August 1919*, vol. 4 (Cambridge, 1966), p. 99.
7. Smuts, "Report," ibid., p. 933.
8. Smuts, "Peace Making," ibid., p. 932.
9. "Editorial," *Le Temps*, 10 April 1919.
10. E. Varga, *La Dictature du Proletariat: Problèmes Economiques* (Paris, 1922), p. 49. See also Lazitch and Drachkovitch, *Lenin and the Comintern*, p. 116.
11. V.I. Lenin, "To Bela Kun," *Collected Works*, vol. 36, p. 542.
12. V.I. Lenin, "Record of Wireless Message to Bela Kun, 23 March 1919," *Collected Works*, vol. 29, p. 227.
13. For Bela Kun's autonomous initiatives, see Lazitch and Drachkovitch, *Lenin and the Comintern*, pp. 118–119.
14. Ibid., pp. 119 ff.

15. I. Silone, "Come Ricordo Lenin," *Corriere della Sera*, 22 April 1970, p. 3. Silone recounted the anecdote a second time in the *Corriere della Sera*, 21 January 1974, p. 3. In 1921, Lenin told Clara Zetkin that Bela Kun was a dreamer who always felt obliged to be "more to the Left than the Left." See C. Zetkin, *Reminiscences of Lenin* (New York, 1934), p. 23.
16. Cf. Lazitch and Drachkovitch, *Lenin and the Comintern*, pp. 117–118.
17. V.I. Lenin, "Telegram to I.I. Vatsetis and S.I. Aralov," *Collected Works*, vol. 44, p. 215. The text of the telegram reads: "The advance into part of Galicia and Bukovina is essential for contact with Soviet Hungary. This task must be achieved more quickly and surely, but beyond this task no occupation of Galicia and Bukovina is needed, for Ukrainian army must on no account be distracted from its two main objectives: the first, the most important and most urgent, is to help the Donets Basin. This assistance must be given quickly and on a large scale. The second objective is to establish a secure link by rail with Soviet Hungary. Inform us of your directives to Antonov and measures for checking their fulfillment."
18. V.I. Lenin, "To Bela Kun," *Collected Works*, vol. 44, p. 271.

Chapter 11

1. FRUS, *1919, Russia*, p. 62.
2. Fischer, *The Soviets in World Affairs*, p. 323.
3. Farnsworth, *William Bullitt and the Soviet Union*, p. 48.
4. E.H. Carr, *The Bolshevik Revolution, 1917–1923*, vol. 3 (London, 1953), pp. 309–310.
5. Ibid., p. 311.
6. F. von Rabenau, *Seeckt: Aus seinem Leben, 1918–1936* (Leipzig, 1940), p. 252. Von Seeckt repeated in a memorandum, 11 September 1922, that Germany would not be bolshevized by an agreement with Russia on foreign affairs (see pp. 315–318; this text was also published in *Der Monat*, November 1948, pp. 43–47).
7. Carr, *The Bolshevik Revolution, 1917–1923*, vol. 3, p. 310.
8. L. Kochan, *Russia and the Weimar Republic* (Cambridge, England, 1954), pp. 22–24; and Freund, *Unholy Alliance*, pp. 50–51.
9. Victor Kopp, who had been fighting in the czarist army during World War I, was taken prisoner by the Germans in 1915. In 1918, he was freed upon special request of the Soviet Embassy in Berlin. Immediately thereafter, he entered the Russian diplomatic corps. See J. Korbel, *Poland between East and West: Soviet and German Diplomacy toward Poland, 1919–1933* (Princeton, N.J., 1963), pp. 76–77.
10. For Enver Pasha, see the bibliographical note written by A. Karahan in *Encyclopedie de l'Islam*, 2d ed. Karl Radek had been among those who suggested that Enver go to Moscow. Cf. Radek, "November," in Carr, "Radek's 'Political Salon,'" p. 420. For the relationship between Radek and Enver, see below, chapter 12.
11. DBFP 1919–1939, vol. 2, pp. 44 ff. See also Kochan, *Russia and the Weimar Republic*, pp. 20–21. For the relations between the Junkers factory and the Soviets, see Carr, *The Bolshevik Revolution, 1917–1923*, vol. 3, p. 436.

12. Kochan, *Russia and the Weimar Republic*, p. 17; and Fischer, *Men and Politics*, p. 129. In September 1920, Enver Pasha took part in the "Conference of Oppressed Peoples" organized by the Soviets in Baku.
13. Korbel, *Poland between East and West*, pp. 76–78.
14. See "Editorial," *Le Temps*, 2 November 1919.
15. X. Joukoff Eudin and H.H. Fisher in collaboration with R. Brown Jones, eds., *Soviet Russia and the West, 1920–1927: A Documentary Survey* (Stanford, 1967), p. 25. See also Kochan, *Russia and the Weimar Republic*, pp. 24–25.
16. Seeckt Papers, St. Antony's Collection, microfilm, reel 21, doc. 111, The National Archives, Washington, D.C. For further developments of von Seeckt's pro-Soviet attitude, see below, chapter 17.

Chapter 12

1. See above, chapter 5.
2. K. Radek, "November," in Carr, "Radek's 'Political Salon,'" p. 419.
3. Ibid.
4. For Radek's conversations with Rathenau, Harden, von Reibnitz, Bauer, and von Hintze, see ibid., pp. 420–422 and 425–427.
5. Fischer, *Stalin and German Communism*, pp. 206–207.
6. See above, chapter 5.
7. *Bulletin Communiste*, 22 April 1930, p. 13. See also Lazitch and Drachkovitch, *Lenin and the Comintern*, pp. 99–100.
8. Radek's letter is reprinted in the introduction to A. Paquet, *Der Geist der Russischen Revolution* (Leipzig, 1919). See also Broué, *Rivoluzione in Germania, 1917–1923*, pp. 275–277.
9. A. Mitchell, *Revolution in Bavaria, 1918–1919: The Eisner Regime and the Soviet Republic* (Princeton, N.J., 1965), p. 308.
10. N. Zastenker, "Bavaraskaia Sovetskaia Respublika i Taktika Kommunistov,"*Istorik Marksist* (Moscow) 4–5 (26–27), 1932, p. 247; quoted in Lazitch and Drachkovitch, *Lenin and the Comintern*, pp. 103–104.
11. V.I. Lenin, "Message of Greetings to the Bavarian Soviet Republic," *Collected Works*, vol. 29, pp. 325–326. This is how Lenin greeted the Bavarian republic of soviets:
    We thank you for your message of greetings, and on our part wholeheartedly greet the Soviet republic of Bavaria. We ask you insistently to give us more frequent, definite information on the following. What measures have you taken to fight the bourgeois executioners, the Scheidemanns and Co.; have councils of workers and servants been formed in the different sections of the city; have the workers been armed; have the bourgeoisie been disarmed; has use been made of the stocks of clothing and other items for immediate and extensive aid to workers, and especially to the farm laborers and small peasants; have the capitalist factories and wealth in Munich and the capitalist farm in its environs been confiscated; have mortgage and rent payments by small peasants been cancelled; have the wages of farm laborers and unskilled workers been doubled or trebled; have all paper stocks and all printing-presses been confiscated so as

to enable popular leaflets and newspapers to be printed for the masses; has the six-hour working day with two- or three-hour instruction in state administration been introduced; have the bourgeoisie in Munich been made to give up surplus housing so that workers may be immediately moved into comfortable flats; have you taken over all the banks; have you taken hostages from the ranks of the bourgeoisie; have you introduced higher rations for the workers than for the bourgeoisie; have all the workers been mobilised for defence and for ideological propaganda in the neighboring villages?

12. K. Radek, *Zur Taktik des Kommunismus: Ein Schreiben an den Oktober-Parteitag der KPD* (Hamburg, 1919), pp. 9–12.
13. Radek, "November," in Carr, "Radek's 'Political Salon,'" p. 425. In the name of the Soviet government, Kopp proposed that the Germans exchange Radek for several hostages.
14. For Lenin's opinion of Bukharin, see above, chapter 4. For Bukharin's criticism of the letter drawn up by Radek, Levi and Clara Zetkin, see *Krasnaja Nov'* 10 (1926): 171–172.
15. *Manchester Guardian*, 8 January 1920, p. 7.
16. *Izvestiia*, 29 January 1920. Cf. Dennis, *The Foreign Policy of Soviet Russia*, pp. 358–359; and Carr, *The Bolshevik Revolution, 1917–1923*, vol. 3, p. 321.

CHAPTER 13

1. V.I. Lenin, "To Comrade Serrati and to All Italian Communists," *Collected Works*, vol. 30, pp. 91–92. The letter was printed originally in *Avanti!* (Piedmont edition), 6 December 1919.
2. Balabanoff, *Lenin Visto da Vicino*, pp. 118–119.
3. G. Salvemini, "Lezioni di Harvard: L'Italia dal 1919 al 1929," in *Scritti sul Fascismo*, vol. 1, ed. R. Vivarelli (Milan, 1961), pp. 494–495.
4. R. Forges Davanzati, "Editorial," *L' Idea Nazionale*, 8 December 1919. See also "La Lettera di Lenin," *Comunismo*, 15 and 31 December 1919, p. 408.
5. *La Giustizia*, 25 July 1920, pp. 1–2.
6. For Serrati's letter, see *Rinascita*, 3 February 1967.
7. Radek, "November," in Carr, "Radek's 'Political Salon,'" p. 424.
8. *Avanti!*, 7 February 1920.
9. *Camera dei Deputati: Discussioni*, Session of 7 February 1920, pp. 999–1000. For Nitti's policies, see E. Serra, *Nitti e la Russia* (Bari, 1975); and G. Petracchi, *La Russia Rivoluzionaria nella Politica Italiana: Le Relazioni Italo-Sovietiche, 1917–1925* (Rome-Bari, 1982).
10. *L'Idea Nazionale*, 13 December 1919.
11. *Camera dei Deputati: Discussioni*, Session of 13 December 1919, p. 269.
12. DVP SSSR, vol. 2, p. 319. The text of Chicherin's telegram was retransmitted by journalist Arturo Cappa to Rome's newspaper *Il Tempo*, 14 March 1920. Cf. ACS, Presidenza, 19.29.9, folder 207.
13. In a speech Lenin gave on 19 December, he stated that a turning point had been reached in the international situation in which the Western bourgeoisie was no longer able to keep up the "blockade" against Soviet Russia because of the opposition of the working class:

> Perhaps the most vivid expression of the turn that has come in the politics of the European countries is the voting of the deputies in the Italian chamber which we know of from the report sent by wireless from France to America and picked up by our wireless station. The report was this. When the question of Russia was discussed in the Italian chamber, and when the socialists proposed the immediate recognition of the Soviet republic, a hundred voted for and two hundred against the proposal; that means that only the workers were in favor of recognizing the Soviet republic and all the bourgeois deputies rejected it. After that, however, the Italian chamber passed a unanimous motion to the effect that the Italian government approach the Allies with a view to stop the blockade altogether and put an end to all intervention in Russian affairs. That was a decision adopted by a chamber that consists to the extent of two-thirds, if not three-quarters, of landowners and capitalists, that was adopted in one of the victor countries and that was adopted simply under pressure from the working-class movement.
>
> See V.I. Lenin, "Speech at a Meeting in Presnya District on the Anniversary of the December Uprising, 1905, 19 December 1919," *Collected Works*, vol. 30, p. 281.

14. *Le Temps*, 27 and 30 December 1919.
15. Archivio Centrale dello Stato, Ministero degli Interni, Affari Generali e Riservati, Movimento Comunista in Italia e all'Estero, box 4, folder 6. The letter is reprinted in R. Monteleone, "Il Partito Comunista Austriaco: Rapporti e Corrispondenza con gli Italiani nel Primo Dopoguerra," *Movimento Operaio e Socialista*, July-September 1972, p. 82.
16. *Manchester Guardian*, 12 March 1920 (but the interview was dated 27 February 1920). Turati went on to speak of the consumerist habits that the Italian working class was acquiring. Antonio Gramsci also admitted in a famous letter to Zino Zini that in 1919–1920, with a working class "which tended to see things through rose-colored glasses and preferred songs and brass bands to sacrifices," the counterrevolutionaries would be able to sweep revolution away. Gramsci's letter is reprinted in G. Bosio, *La Grande Paura, Settembre 1920: L'Occupazione delle Fabbriche* (Rome, 1970), p. 20.
17. Archivio Centrale dello Stato, Ministero degli Interni, Direzione Generale di Pubblica Sicurezza, Capo della Polizia (Atti Confidenziali), folder "Perri," quoted in Petracchi, *La Russia Rivoluzionaria nella Politica Italiana*, pp. 164–165.
18. ACS, Presidenza, 19.29.9, Missioni Socialiste in Russia, box 206.
19. V.I. Lenin, "On the Struggle within the Italian Socialist Party,"*Collected Works*, vol. 31, p. 387.
20. A. Balabanoff, *La mia Vita di Rivoluzionaria*, pp. 227–228. She had already related the episode in *Ricordi di una Socialista*, pp. 331–332.
21. *La Correspondance Internationale*, 28 November 1922, supplement 25.

Chapter 14

1. Cf. I. Spector, *The First Russian Revolution: Its Impact on Asia* (Englewood Cliffs, N.J., 1962).
2. Fischer, *The Soviets in World Affairs*, p. 17.

3. X. Joukoff Eudin and R.C. North, eds., *Soviet Russia and the East, 1920–1927: A Documentary Survey* (Stanford, 1964), p. 77–78; and J.V. Stalin, "Don't Forget the East," *Works*, vol. 4, pp. 174–176.
4. On 19 February, the king of Afghanistan was mysteriously killed and his heir, Amanullah, declared war on Great Britain, recognized Soviet Russia, and sent a delegation to Moscow. On 6 May, the head of this delegation, Professor Bakatullah, in an interview for *Izvestiia*, stated that he was neither communist nor socialist, but that he was willing to ally himself with the communists in order to chase all the English out of Asia. Cf. Joukoff Eudin and North, *Soviet Russia and the East*, p. 83.
5. J.M. Meijer, ed., *The Trotsky Papers, 1917–1922*, vol. 1 (London, The Hague, and Paris, 1964), pp. 620–627.
6. G.V. Chicherin, "Rossiia i Aziatskie Narodny," in *Vestnik Narodnogo Kommissariata po Inostrannym Delam*, 12 August 1919, p. 7; quoted in Joukoff Eudin and North, *Soviet Russia and the East*, p. 83.
7. Balabanoff, *Lenin Visto da Vicino*, pp. 94–95.
8. V.I. Lenin, "Address to the Second All-Russia Congress of Communist Organizations of the Peoples of the East, 22 November 1919," *Collected Works*, vol. 30, pp. 161–162. In 1913, Lenin had claimed that while the bourgeoisie in Europe was reactionary, the bourgeoisie in Asia was revolutionary. See V.I. Lenin, "Backward Europe and Advanced Asia, 18 May 1913," *Collected Works*, vol. 19, pp. 99–100.
9. V.I. Lenin, "Report of the Commission on the National and Colonial Questions, 26 July 1920," *Collected Works*, vol. 31, p. 244.
10. Fischer, *The Soviets in World Affairs*, pp. 335–337.
11. Joukoff Eudin and North, *Soviet Russia and the East*, pp. 91–100. According to Fischer, *Men and Politics*, p. 136, Kucik Kahn, one of the heads of the republic of Gilan, after the defeat at the hands of Reza Kahn, fled into the mountains where he subsequently died of exposure. His body was found by Reza's men and his head was carried through the streets of Teheran. Stalin, who had supported Kucik Kahn, was infuriated. His rage was particularly directed at Soviet representative in Teheran Fyodor Rothstein, considered to be responsible for this death and, more generally, for the end of the republic of Gilan. The issue was raised in a Politburo meeting, and Lenin, impatient with the discussion, tried to cut it off with the comment, "Well. Sharp reprimand to comrade Rothstein for having killed Kucik Kahn." Someone objected that Kucik had been killed by Reza Kahn, and Lenin replied, "Well. Sharp reprimand to Reza." Stalin reminded him that they could not send a reprimand to Reza since he was not a Soviet citizen. At that, Lenin broke out in laughter along with several others. The group then went on to discuss other matters. Fischer wrote that this episode was told to him by "someone present at the meeting."
12. For Russian-Afghan relations, see Joukoff Eudin and North, *Soviet Russia and the East*, pp. 83, 103–105, 183 passim; Fischer, *The Soviets in World Affairs*, pp. 331–333; Fischer, *Men and Politics*, pp. 144–145 and 150–151; P.T. Etherton, *In the Heart of Asia* (Boston and New York, 1926), pp. 233 passim. Both the Russians and the British offered Afghanistan a treaty of alliance. But the Afghans, preferring to remain unaligned, signed only friendship treaties. See W.K. Fraser-Tytler, *Afghanistan: A Study of Political Developments in Central Asia* (London, 1950), p. 199.

13. Fischer, *The Soviets in World Affairs*, pp. 460–464; Joukoff Eudin and North, *Soviet Russia and the East*, pp. 113–114.

Chapter 15

1. Cf. M. Gilbert, *Winston S. Churchill*, vol. 4 (London, 1975), pp. 268–269, 304–305 and 327.
2. E.M. Carroll, *Soviet Communism and Western Opinion, 1919–1921*, ed. F.B.M. Holliday (Chapel Hill, 1965), pp. 51–52.
3. Rowland, *Lloyd George*, pp. 501–504. In his letter to Churchill, Lloyd George made the observation that a victory of a former czarist general could cause tensions in the Baltic regions where new nations had been founded thanks to the downfall of the czarist regime. In other words, support given to the White forces brought with it certain risks that Great Britain did not want to incur. Cf. M.L. Dockrill and J. Douglas Goold, *Peace Without Promise: Britain and the Peace Conferences, 1919–1923* (London, 1981), pp. 113–118.
4. In October 1919, when the Secretariat of the Supreme Council of the Allies asked Germany and other neutral nations to join in the "blockade," it became clear that none of these countries intended to assent. See Carr, *The Bolshevik Revolution, 1917–1923*, vol. 3, pp. 149–150. Menshevik leader I. Martov was among those to state that a resumption of trade would increase the possibility of change in Russian government. See Levine, *Eyewitness to History*, p. 74.
5. For Malone's mission, see above, chapter 8.
6. *Times* (London), 10 November 1919, p. 15; and *Le Temps*, 10 November 1919, p. 2.
7. *The Parliamentary Debates: Official Report*, Fifth Series, vol. 121, p. 474.
8. Ibid., p. 723. Lloyd George was referring not only to the threat of Bolshevik Russia, but also to that of the White Russians, since they were determined to re-establish the empire along its old borders.
9. DBFP 1919–1939, vol. 3, pp. 593, 643–644 and 661.
10. For Litvinov's credentials, see ibid., pp. 671–672.
11. The document is reprinted in Dennis, *The Foreign Policies of Soviet Russia*, p. 380.
12. DBFP 1919–1939, vol. 3, pp. 643–645.
13. Ibid., pp. 663–666 and 670–671 passim. See also *Le Temps*, 3–5 December 1919.
14. DVP SSSR, vol. 2, pp. 298–299 and 306–308. The Soviet document is reprinted in Degras, *Soviet Documents on Foreign Policy*, pp. 176–177.
15. DBFP 1919–1939, vol. 3, pp. 738–740. Litvinov wrote about economic problems:

> I need not dwell upon the advantages which would accrue to all countries from renewed intercourse with Russia, but there is no getting away from the facts that Great Britain is in need of flax and other raw materials accumulating in Russia, and that Russia in her turn could absorb enormous quantities of British manufactured goods. The Soviet government is disposed to consider favorably any suggestions on the part of British industry and finance for placing economic relations between the two countries on a sound basis.

16. Cf. Carroll, *Soviet Communism and Western Opinion*, pp. 30–31.
17. DBFP 1919–1939, vol. 3, pp. 747–748.
18. On 19 March, Lenin said, "We must arrange things so that the German traitor-socialists will not be able to say that the Bolsheviks are trying to impose their universal system which, as it were, can be brought into Berlin on Red Army bayonets." See V.I. Lenin, "Eighth Congress of the R.C.P. (B.), Report on the Party Program, 18–23 March 1919," *Collected Works*, vol. 29, p. 74.
19. Radek had met with both Talaat Pasha and Enver Pasha. See above, chapter 12.
20. Lord A.C. Northcliffe, British press magnate, founded the *Daily Mail* in 1896 and the *Daily Mirror* in 1903.

CHAPTER 16

1. *Le Temps*, 25 December 1919, p. 2.
2. V.I. Lenin, "Decision of the Politbureau of the C.C., R.C.P. (B.) in Connection with the Entente's Attempt to Start Trade Relations with Russia through the Russian Co-operatives," *Collected Works*, vol. 42, p. 159.
3. V.I. Lenin, "Interview with Lincoln Eyre, Correspondent of the American Newspaper the *World*," ibid., pp. 175–180.
4. *Le Temps*, 26 February 1920, p. 1. On 25 February, Chicherin telegraphed Washington that the Soviet government, "having no intention whatever of interfering with the internal affairs of America and having for its sole aim peace and trade," desired to open negotiations with the White House. See FRUS, *1920*, vol. 3, p. 447.
5. Fischer, *The Soviets in World Affairs*, p. 251. The Western Allies were well aware of the substance of the problem of the cooperatives. A report by two Italian envoys, Virginio Gayda and Michail Koblinsky, sent from Copenhaghen on 11 April, after a meeting with Litvinov, stated: "It must be understood that Russia accepted the pretence of the cooperatives as proposed by the Entente governments. But these cooperatives are now institutions of the Russian state and, therefore, dealing with them means *de facto* dealing with the Soviet government." See ASMAE, AA.PP., Russia, f. 1522 bis.
6. V.I. Lenin, "Speech at a Meeting of the Railwaymen of Moscow Junction, 5 February 1920," *Collected Works*, vol. 30, p. 345; and "Report on the Work of the All-Russia Central Executive Committee of the Council of People's Commissars Delivered at the First Session of the All-Russia Central Executive Committee, 7th Convocation, 2 February 1920," ibid., p. 317.
7. "Editorial," *Le Temps*, 5 February 1920, p. 1. The readers of *Le Temps* were made to understand the harsh reality behind the positive, superficial appearances of Bolshevism. The article stated:

> Bolshevik Russia achieved her victory by turning her back on the theories she had proclaimed. A proletarian party took into its service the officers, the officials, and the police of the old regime. A revolutionary party established a type of despotism that was more rigid than that of the Czar. An internationalist party re-created a unified Russia. And when Lenin deals with the *bourgeois* government of Estonia or offers a peace agreement to the *bourgeois* government

of Poland, he is not acting as an apostle of revolution but as the head of a Russian government established in Moscow.
8. *The Parliamentary Debates: Official Report*, Fifth Series, vol. 125, pp. 43 and 89. In the Italian Chamber of Deputies, Prime Minister Nitti expressed similar ideas: "I am convinced that the Russian government, as a result of direct relations with Europe after all the isolation, will end up absorbing a moderating influence." See *Atti Parlamentari, Camera dei Deputati, Discussioni*, Session of 7 February 1920, pp. 999–1000. On 9 March, the newspaper *Epoca* printed an interview with Minister of Industry Dante Ferraris, who declared:

> If Bolshevism has as much vitality and force as the socialists have been assuring us, it is a kind of paradise. Then, why shouldn't we have our share of this paradise? If instead, it is something quite different — a kind of hell — we must get to know it better here in the West, so that it does not give rise to dangerous illusions in the masses. If Bolshevism has not got all the force and vitality attributed to it from afar, it will become corrupted and will dissolve upon contact with Western civilization. The civilization which is superior will prevail through forces above and beyond our own will.

9. DBFP 1919–1939, vol. 7, pp. 140 ff. See also R.H. Ullman, *The Anglo-Soviet Accord* (Princeton, N.J., 1972), pp. 29–31.
10. *Times* (London), 25 February 1920.
11. Cf. Ullman, *The Anglo-Soviet Accord*, p. 36.
12. Ibid., p. 41.
13. Ibid., pp. 43–45 and 91. For the minutes of the meetings of the San Remo Conference, 18–26 April 1920, see DBFP 1919–1939, vol. 8, 1920.
14. Bombacci did not want to be the one to put his signature on the agreements with Litvinov. If he signed in the government's name, everyone would realize that coming to agreement with the Bolsheviks was enough to turn the most violent revolutionaries into faithful government agents. But the atmosphere prevailing in Italy during that period was one of general pacification, beginning with foreign relations and spreading to internal affairs. Under-Secretary of Foreign Affairs Count Sforza telegraphed the Italian minister in Copenhagen on 6 March: "You can communicate the arrival of Bombacci as representative of our cooperative institutions, but not giving the fact importance. We want the trip to take place for economic reasons." In a 9 April telegram to Brigatti Tedeschi, a member of the legation to Copenhagen, Count Sforza wrote: "Please inform Bombacci that the Prime Minister approves the draft of the accord. You and Bombacci are asked to sign in the name of the government." Both telegrams are in ASMAE, AA.PP., Russia, f. 1522 bis. See also Petracchi, *La Russia Rivoluzionaria nella Politica Italiana*, pp. 169 passim.
15. For Gayda's and Kobilinsky's reports from Copenhagen, April 1920, see ASMAE, AA.PP., Russia, f. 1522 bis; and Serra, *Nitti e la Russia*, pp. 86 ff. See also the aforementioned interview with Minister Dante Ferraris, *Epoca*, 9 March 1920.
16. Petracchi, *La Russia Rivoluzionaria nella Politica Italiana*, p. 160. In May 1920, professor Campa organized a series of lectures in Moscow on Italian culture. They were opened by Commissar for Education Lunacharski.
17. Telegram to the Italian Legation in Copenhagen, 12 April 1920, ASMAE, AA.PP., Russia, f. 1522 bis.

18. V.I. Lenin, "Speech Delivered at the First (Inaugural) All-Russia Congress of Mineworkers," *Collected Works*, vol. 30, p. 496.

CHAPTER 17

1. Korbel, *Poland between East and West*, pp. 23–25, 37 and 61–62; Carroll, *Soviet Communism and Western Opinion*, pp. 58–69; and Carr, *The Bolshevik Revolution, 1917–1923*, vol. 3, pp. 154–155.
2. V.I. Lenin, "Speech Delivered at the First All-Russian Congress of Working Cossaks, 1 March 1920," *Collected Works*, vol. 30, p. 394.
3. L. Trotsky, *Stalin: An Appraisal of the Man and his Influence* (New York and London, 1941), p. 328.
4. Trotsky, *My Life*, p. 457.
5. Ibid., p. 456.
6. V.I. Lenin, "To the C.C. of the R.C.P. (B.)," *Collected Works*, vol. 44, p. 200.
7. See W. Lerner, "Poland in 1920: A Case Study in Foreign-Policy Decision Making under Lenin," *South Atlantic Quarterly* 72, n. 3 (Summer 1973): 409.
8. V.I. Lenin, "Speech Delivered at a Congress of Leather Industry Workers, 2 October 1920," *Collected Works*, vol. 31, p. 305. See also Carr, *The Bolshevik Revolution, 1917–1923*, vol. 3, p. 325: "According to an unpublished memorandum of Reibnitz written about 1940, extracts from which have been communicated to me by Mr. Gustav Hilger, Reibnitz negotiated with Radek and Kopp at this time a plan under which, as soon as the Red Army entered Warsaw, German *Freikorps* detachments would advance in West Prussia and Upper Silesia as far as the old German frontier."
9. An unsuccessful putsch in Germany led by Wolfgang Kapp constituted a hard blow for the anti-Bolshevik factions and reinforced the positions of von Seeckt and von Schleicher, the promoters of an accord with Bolshevik Russia as well as enemies of the Polish nation. See E.H. Carr, *German-Soviet Relations between the Two World Wars, 1919–1939* (Baltimore, 1951), p. 31.
10. F. von Rabenau, *Seeckt: Aus seinem Leben, 1918–1936*, p. 252.
11. Seeckt Papers, reel 21, doc. 111. For Seeckt's declarations, see above, chapter 11, note 6. General von Seeckt asserted in a memorandum, 26 February 1920, that if the Soviets succeeded in invading Poland, the German state would be able to free itself from the harsh conditions imposed by the Versailles treaty. Cf. Korbel, *Poland between East and West*, pp. 73–74.
12. For the discussions with the two Soviet emissaries, see memorandum, 9 February 1920, microfilm, reel 33, doc. AS 261, St. Antony's Collection, The National Archives, Washington, D.C.; and memorandum, 11 February 1920, ibid., doc. AS 272 b. See also Korbel, *Poland between East and West*, pp. 28–30. On 8 August, French Premier Millerand informed Lloyd George that France would invade the Rhineland if Germany attacked Poland. Cf. DBFP 1919–1939, vol. 8, p. 712. Chicherin had sent a message to Litvinov on 14 February, reporting that word was going round about the desire expressed by German military circles to join with the Soviets against Poland. "We do not approve this policy," the Russian Commissar noted. He added that if the Poles, who were not taking enough notice

of the German peril, should attack Russia, they would risk finding themselves caught between two swords. According to Chicherin, proof existed that the Germans were making preparations to attack Poland, and he urged the press to make this danger known to the Poles. See DVP SSSR, vol. 2, pp. 370–371.

13. R. Himmer, "Soviet Policy toward Germany during the Russo-Polish War, 1920," *Slavic Review*, (December 1976): 671–672. See also Kochan, *Russia and the Weimar Republic*, p. 24.
14. In March 1920, von Seeckt asked a close aide, Major Friedrich von Bötticher, to draw up a memorandum which clearly called for a German alliance with Russia and a repartitioning of Poland. See Seeckt Papers, reel 22, doc. 149. See also Korbel, *Poland between East and West*, pp. 74–75.
15. St. Antony's Collection, microfilm, reel 3925, doc. K. 28, 095851–3. See also Himmer, "Soviet Policy toward Germany during the Russo-Polish War, 1920," p. 672.
16. Hilger and Meyer, *The Incompatible Allies*, pp. 25–26.
17. Carr, *The Bolshevik Revolution, 1917–1923*, vol. 3, p. 325. On 22 July, the *Rote Fahne*, a publication of the German Communist party, reported that the Soviets would never cross the borders of the Reich nor supply military assistance to a revolution in Germany. This article is quoted in Carroll, *Soviet Communism and Western Opinion*, pp. 142 and 270. The same day, the German Minister of Foreign Affairs sent the Soviets a letter urging further diplomatic contacts, to which Chicherin replied affirmatively on 2 August. Cf. DVP SSSR, vol. 3, pp. 75–78. For Lenin's resentment against Kopp, see below, chapter 19.
18. *Corriere della Sera*, 28 July 1920.
19. Ambassador De Martino's telegram, 30 July 1920, ASMAE, Telegrammi in Arrivo, vol. 71. Ambassador De Martino became more and more convinced that secret agreements existed between the Germans and the Soviets. "It seems to me quite likely that accords exist," he stated, "consistent with the various tendencies regarding the Soviets. These agreements, though they may well not be formally signed, are valid and efficient, since they are based on common political and economic interests." See telegram, 6 August 1920, ibid. Also on 6 August, *Le Temps* stated that the Soviet-German alliance was an accomplished fact. Cf. *Corriere della Sera*, 7 August 1920, p. 4. The German authorities arrested Bela Kun at the end of July, and yet Foreign Minister Simons declared that the head of the Hungarian communists was free to go to Moscow. See Carroll, *Soviet Communism and Western Opinion*, p. 14. At the same time, Gustav Stresemann was worrying that the Russians might occupy the ex-German territories of Poland. Cf. ibid., p. 151. However, General von Seeckt affirmed that even if that happened, Germany ought not to join with Poland. See memorandum, 31 July 1920, Seeckt Papers, microfilm, reel 21. See also H. von Riekhoff, *German-Polish Relations, 1918–1933* (Baltimore and London, 1971), p. 32.
20. C.F. Melville, *The Russian Face of Germany: An Account of the Secret Military Relations between the German and Soviet-Russian Governments* (London, 1932), p. 41. The German citizens of Prostken, on the border with Poland, organized military units to fight side by side with the Russians, and similar occurrences also took place elsewhere. Cf. Korbel, *Poland between East and West*, pp. 89–90.
21. Carroll, *Soviet Communism and Western Opinion*, pp. 138 and 269.
22. V.I. Lenin, "Speech Delivered at the Ninth All-Russia Conference of the Russian

Communist Party (B.), 22 September 1920," *Collected Works*, vol. 31, p. 276.
23. V.I. Lenin, "Report on Concessions Delivered at the R.C.P. (B.) Groups at the Eighth Congress of Soviets, 21 December 1920," *Collected Works*, vol. 31, pp. 475–477.

CHAPTER 18

1. For the lack of British aid to Poland, see Ullman, *The Anglo-Soviet Accord*, pp. 50 ff. For Nitti's order, see Serra, *Nitti e la Russia*, pp. 128–129. Some aid did reach Poland from the West, and the French sent General Weigand. But basically, the Poles had to rely on their own efforts.
2. This refers to the proposal Paderewski made in September 1919. See above, chapter 15.
3. Carroll, *Soviet Communism and Western Opinion*, p. 56.
4. Ibid., pp. 60–61; and DBFP 1919–1939, vol. 3, pp. 803–805.
5. *The Parliamentary Debates: Official Report*, Fifth Series, vol. 125, pp. 41 ff. See also S.R. Graubard, *British Labour and the Russian Revolution, 1917–1924* (Cambridge, Mass., 1956), p. 90.
6. For the San Remo Conference (18–26 April 1920), see above, chapter 16. The French were not strong enough to successfully oppose the British Prime Minister on his Russian policy. They were particularly ill at ease at the San Remo Conference because, on 6 April, they had sent their troops to occupy Frankfurt without consulting the Allies. Cf. Carroll, *Soviet Communism and Western Opinion*, p. 46.
7. G.A. Riddell, *Lord Riddell's Intimate Diary of the Peace Conference and after, 1918–1923* (London, 1933), p. 197. Great Britain, too, was running serious risks because of Russia during that period. On 28 April, the Bolsheviks founded the Soviet republic of Azerbaijan; in May, divisions of the Red Army landed at Enzeli, Persia; on 4 June, the socialist republic of Gilan was set up. For these events, see above, chapter 14.
8. Ibid., pp. 191 ff. On 30 May, when Polish troops occupied Kiev, Lloyd George said to Lord Riddell: "The Poles have quarrelled with all their neighbours, and they are a menace to the peace of Europe." See ibid., p. 198.
9. DVP SSSR, vol. 2, pp. 502–503.
10. DBFP 1919–1939, vol. 12, n. 703.
11. Ullman, *The Anglo-Soviet Accord*, p. 97.
12. DBFP 1919–1939, vol. 8, pp. 180–192.
13. Minutes of the meeting of 7 June 1920, ibid., vol. 8, pp. 292–306. See also Ullman, *The Anglo-Soviet Accord*, p. 104.
14. The report is published in *Avanti!*, 9 September 1920, p. 1.
15. Note by Lenin attached to Trotsky's memorandum, 4 June 1920, Trotsky Archives, Houghton Library, Harvard University, folder T-533. See also Ullman, *The Anglo-Soviet Accord*, pp. 162–163.
16. V.I. Lenin, "To G.V. Chicherin," *Collected Works*, vol. 44, p. 386.
17. Telegram from Chicherin to Krasin, 12 June 1920, intercepted by the British; quoted in Ullman, *The Anglo-Soviet Accord*, pp. 116–117. Two days later, Chiche-

rin telegraphed Curzon that Litvinov would be better qualified than Krasin to deal with political questions. See DBFP 1919–1939, vol. 12, p. 737.
18. DVP SSSR, vol. 2, pp. 638–661; and Ullman, *The Anglo-Soviet Accord*, pp. 164–165. In Chicherin's report of 17 June, he also discussed relations with France, Italy, and other nations. The Foreign Commissar stated that although England wanted reconciliation, France opposed it and was supported by certain elements in the British government. Chicherin held the view that France would not be able to prevent an accord. He considered Italy's policy to be "enigmatic" and lacking in autonomy.
19. Record of this meeting is found only in Lloyd George Papers, Beaverbrook Library, London, F. 202.3.19, quoted in Ullman, *The Anglo-Soviet Accord*, p. 105.
20. Ullman, *The Anglo-Soviet Accord*, p. 110.
21. DBFP 1919–1939, vol. 8, pp. 323 ff.
22. Telegram from Chicherin to Krasin, 18 June 1920, intercepted by the British; quoted in Ullman, *The Anglo-Soviet Accord*, p. 118.
23. Telegram from Chicherin to Krasin, 25 June 1920, intercepted by the British; ibid., pp. 121–122.
24. Ibid.
25. Krasin himself expressed his difficulties as a negotiator to Lloyd George. See minutes of the meeting of 29 June 1920, DBFP 1919–1939, vol. 8, p. 380.
26. Telegram from Chicherin to Krasin, 26 June 1920, intercepted by the British; quoted in Ullman, *The Anglo-Soviet Accord*, pp. 123–124.
27. Foreign Secretary Curzon was among those against an accord with the Bolsheviks. On 12 June, Winston Churchill, Minister of War at that time, told Lord Riddell that profound differences of opinion existed between Lloyd George and himself regarding Russia. See Riddell, *Lord Riddell's Intimate Diary*, p. 203.
28. V.I. Lenin, "Letter to the British Workers, 30 May 1920," *Collected Works*, vol. 31, p. 142.
29. The *New Statesman*, 19 June 1920, described Lenin's letter as "an almost incredibly inept piece of work. Its crude violence, its tone of contemptuous condescension, its doctrinaire shibboleths . . . in short, nearly every one of its features, might have been expressly designed by some subtle enemy to discredit its writer in the sight not only of the ordinary British workingman but even of those enthusiastic left-wingers who have hitherto been proud to dub themselves 'Bolsheviks.'" See Carroll, *Soviet Communism and Western Opinion*, p. 94. Lloyd George confided to Lord Riddell that he found Lenin's letter senseless. Riddell replied that, in his opinion, Lenin was becoming a bit "rattled." See Riddell, *Lord Riddell's Intimate Diary*, p. 204.
30. DBFP 1919–1939, vol. 8, pp. 380 ff.
31. Ullman, *The Anglo-Soviet Accord*, pp. 129–130.
32. DVP SSSR, vol. 3, pp. 16–17.

CHAPTER 19

1. DBFP 1919–1939, vol. 8, pp. 441–442. See also Ullman, *The Anglo-Soviet Accord*, pp. 145–146. Stanislaw Patek, an ex-Minister of Foreign Affairs, at that time

held the post of Minister without Portfolio in the new government headed by W. Grabsky.
2. DBFP 1919–1939, vol. 8, pp. 502–506.
3. Ibid., pp. 490–491.
4. Ibid., pp. 513–518. Italy, which was in total agreement with the content of the note, abstained from signing it solely to avoid embarrassing France. See ibid., p. 516.
5. Meijer, *The Trotsky Papers, 1917–1922*, vol. 2, pp. 228–231.
6. V.I. Lenin, "Telephone Message to J.V. Stalin, 12 or 13 July 1920," *Collected Works*, vol. 31, p. 204; and "To Theodore Rothstein, 15 July 1920," *Collected Works*, vol. 44, p. 403.
7. V.I. Lenin, "To E.M. Sklyansky, 12 or 13 July 1920," *Collected Works*, vol. 44, p. 403.
8. V.I. Lenin, "Telegram to J.V. Stalin, 17 July 1920," *Collected Works*, vol. 31, p. 205. Lenin wrote that the Central Committee Plenum had adopted "almost in full" the proposals he had made.
9. DVP SSSR, vol. 3, pp. 47–53; rpt. also in Degras, *Soviet Documents on Foreign Policy*, vol. 1, pp. 194–197.
10. Riddell, *Lord Riddell's Intimate Diary*, p. 221; and Carroll, *Soviet Communism and Western Opinion*, p. 121.
11. Trotsky, *My Life*, p. 457. See also Carr, *The Bolshevik Revolution, 1917–1923*, pp. 209–210.
12. V.I. Lenin, "To G.V. Chicherin, 22 July 1920," *Collected Works*, vol. 35, p. 452.
13. Himmer, "Soviet Policy toward Germany during the Russo-Polish War, 1920," p. 677. On 12 August, von Maltzan wrote in a memorandum that Bolshevik Russia was not interested in an accord with Germany. See ibid., p. 678.
14. The French and the British Prime Ministers met to discuss the Polish situation on 8 and 9 August. The minutes of these talks confirm that Millerand and Lloyd George were aware of the possibility of a Russian-German accord at the expense of Poland. Millerand stated that if the Germans entered Poland, the Allies would have to retaliate by invading the Rhineland regions. See DBFP 1919–1939, vol. 8, pp. 712–713.
15. Ibid., pp. 649–650. Lloyd George's telegram to the Soviets was also published in the *Times* (London), 26 July 1920.
16. DVP SSSR, vol. 3, pp. 61–64. Chicherin's answer was also published in the *Times* (London), 27 July 1920.
17. Riddell, *Lord Riddell's Intimate Diary*, p. 226.
18. DBFP 1919–1939, vol. 8, pp. 662. See also Ullman, *The Anglo-Soviet Accord*, pp. 190–193.
19. DBFP 1919–1939, vol. 8, pp. 650–651.
20. Ibid., 652 ff. For the Lloyd George-Millerand meeting and for Curzon's proposals, see Ullman, *The Anglo-Soviet Accord*, pp. 189–192.
21. Riddell, *Lord Riddell's Intimate Diary*, p. 227. On 31 July, General von Seeckt wrote that if Soviet Russia accepted the proposal for a conference in London, Germany would take part in the conference as well. See Seeckt Papers, reel 21, doc. 130; and Korbel, *Poland between East and West*, p. 86.
22. DBFP 1919–1939, vol. 8, pp. 670 ff. See also Ullman, *The Anglo-Soviet Accord*, pp. 195 ff.
23. DBFP 1919–1939, vol. 8, pp. 681–708.

24. Ibid., pp. 709 ff.
25. Ibid., p. 735. On 7 August, the secretary of the Labor party, Arthur Henderson, ordered all the trade-union locals around the country to organize demonstrations against the "extremely menacing possibility of an extension of the Polish-Russian War." Throngs of people answered his call and huge demonstrations took place all over the nation. Cf. Coates, *A History of Anglo-Soviet Relations*, p. 42; and Graubard, *British Labour and the Russian Revolution, 1917–1924*, passim.
26. Ullman, *The Anglo-Soviet Accord*, pp. 218–219. The Italian representative in Helsinski, Marchetti Ferrante, sent a telegram to Rome in which he reported on his conversations with Bolshevik spokesmen:

   After my enquiry in Bolshevik circles, I can summarize the situation as follows: the original type of Bolshevism no longer exists in Russia. The Soviet government, convinced that it has reconstructed national unity over the past year, wants to arrive at a peace accord in the position of a major power along with other major powers. The conquest of Poland would give it the opportunity to obtain an advantageous peace agreement. But Moscow is no longer counting on a revolution in Europe, still less in Germany.... For the Russians, bolshevization of Poland is of secondary importance, since a republic of soviets would constitute a weakness in a country considered not ready for communism. The Russian government will certainly want to exploit its success as well as Britain's fears on a diplomatic level. But it does feel the need for peace.

   Telegram n. 4559, 7 August 1920, ASMAE, AA.PP. Finlandia, f. 1039.
27. C.E. Callwell, *Field-Marshal Sir Henry Wilson: His Life and Diaries*, vol. 2 (New York, 1927), p. 256.
28. Ibid., pp. 256–257.
29. Telegram from Kamenev to Chicherin, 6 August 1920, intercepted by the British; quoted in Ullman, *The Anglo-Soviet Accord*, p. 209.
30. Ibid., pp. 228–231.
31. V.I. Lenin, "Telegram to J.V. Stalin, 11 August 1920," *Collected Works*, vol. 31, p. 266.
32. V.I. Lenin, "Telegram to K.K. Danishevsky, 11 August 1920," *Collected Works*, vol. 44, p. 412.
33. V.I. Lenin, "Telegram to I.T. Smilga, 18 August 1920," *Collected Works*, vol. 44, pp. 417–418.
34. V.I. Lenin, "Speech Delivered at the Ninth All-Russia Conference of the Russia Communist Party (B.), 22 September 1920," *Collected Works*, vol. 31, p. 276. Moreover, Lenin said in the "Speech Delivered at a Congress of Leather Industry Workers, 2 October 1920," ibid., p. 305, that by attacking Warsaw, the Russians intended to destroy "the peace of Versailles, on which the whole present system of international relations rests."

Chapter 20

1. The list of nations that were to participate in the London conference is in DBFP 1919–1939, vol. 8, p. 691.
2. Ullman, *The Anglo-Soviet Accord*, pp. 270 ff. Lloyd George continued to provoke conservative circles, and in particular General Wilson, to anger. The latter even

considered the issuing of an anti-government "pronouncement" on the part of the military establishment. See Callwell, *Field-Marshal Sir Henry Wilson*, pp. 259–262.
3. Trotsky is quoted in Fischer, *The Soviets in World Affairs*, p. 301.
4. V.I. Lenin, "Our Foreign and Domestic Position and the Tasks of the Party, Speech Delivered to the Moscow Gubernia Conference of the R.C.P. (B.), 21 November 1920," *Collected Works*, vol. 31, pp. 411–412.
5. Ibid., p. 419.
6. For Bronski's interview, see *Avanti!*, 5 August 1920.
7. As Robert Wohl has rightly remarked about the origins of the French Communist party, Lenin accepted Cachin into the Comintern and rejected Longuet, not because Cachin was the better revolutionary (if anything, the opposite was true), but because Longuet was a man ready to defend his own ideas, who would not have bowed to Moscow's wishes. See R. Wohl, *French Communism in the Making, 1914–1924* (Stanford, 1966), p. 206.
8. Carr, *The Bolshevik Revolution, 1917–1923*, vol. 3, p. 217.
9. For Serrati and Bordiga, see H. Koenig, *Lenin e il Socialismo Italiano, 1915–1921* (Florence, 1972), p. 127. For Roy's position see above, chapter 14. Little by little, the socialists came to realize how self-serving Lenin's policies in the Orient were. See H.N. Brailsford, "La Politica Orientale della Russia," *Avanti!*, 27 January 1921, p. 5. "The Russian threat in the East," Brailsford wrote, "is being carried out with the purpose of convincing the West to recognize the Soviet government and to open trade negotiations with it."
10. For the establishment of the Italian Communist party when the idea of world revolution had already lost its momentum, see P. Spriano, *Storia del Partito Comunista Italiano: Da Bordiga a Gramsci*, vol. 1 (Turin, 1967), pp. 96–97. According to Spriano, "along with the picture of Russia in the clutches of poverty, chaos and a ruthless dictatorship, [in the fall of 1920] there also loomed the shadow of a similar fate for any Western country that should experience revolution. The situation would further deteriorate in France and Italy because the remaining Entente powers would declare an economic blockade on them." Some historians believe that as late as March 1921, Lenin had not discarded the hypothesis of a revolution in Germany. This is not true, as it is clearly demonstrated in the accounts by Zetkin, *Reminiscences of Lenin*, pp. 21 ff.; and Agosti, *La Terza Internazionale*, vol. 1, pp. 335–368.
11. For the journey of the first Italian socialists to Soviet Russia, from May to September 1920, see Melograni, *Fascismo, Comunismo e Rivoluzione Industriale*, pp. 73–82.
12. The nature of communist ideology is clearly outlined in K.D. Bracher, *Zeit der Ideologien* (Stuttgart, 1982).
13. *Avanti!*, 24 November 1919.
14. *Avanti!*, 23 December 1918.
15. Serrati's journal, *Comunismo*, 15 January–15 February 1921, p. 519, immediately considered the party's split that occurred in Livorno a success for reactionary forces. The Italian bourgeoisie, recognizing the split as a victory for itself, believed that it had taken its revenge over the party that had made it tremble so long.

Select Bibliography

UNPUBLISHED DOCUMENTS AND PAPERS

Archivio Centrale dello Stato, Rome, Presidenza del Consiglio dei Ministri, Gabinetto, Serie Speciale, Prima Guerra Mondiale.
Archivio Centrale dello Stato, Rome, Ministero degli Interni, Direzione Generale di Pubblica Sicurezza.
Archivio Storico del Ministero degli Affari Esteri, Rome, Archivio degli Affari Politici.
Seeckt Papers, St. Antony's Collection, [microfilm] The National Archives, Washington, D.C.

PUBLISHED DOCUMENTS AND PAPERS

Agosti, Aldo. *La Terza Internazionale: Storia Documentaria*. Rome: Editori Riuniti, 1974.
Bullitt, William C. *The Bullitt Mission to Russia: Testimony before the Committee on Foreign Relations, United States Senate*. New York, 1919. Rpt. ed., Westport, Ct.: Hyperion, 1977.
Bunyan, James and Fisher, Harold H., eds. *The Bolshevik Revolution, 1917–1918: Documents and Materials*. Stanford: Stanford University Press, 1934.
Camera dei Deputati, *Discussioni*. Rome, 1917–20.
Chicherin, Georgy V. *Two Years of Soviet Foreign Policy*. New York: Russian Soviet Government Bureau, 1920.
Cumming, C.K. and Pettit, Walter W., eds. *Russian American Relations, March 1917–March 1920: Documents and Papers*. New York: Harcourt, Brace and Howe, 1920.
Degras, Jane, ed. *Soviet Documents on Soviet Policy*. London: Oxford University Press, 1951.
Hancok, W.K. and van der Poel, J., eds. *Selection from the Smuts Papers, November 1918–August 1919*. Cambridge: Cambridge University Press, 1966.
Institut Leninizma pri TsK VKP (B). *Protokoly Tsentral'nogo Komiteta RSDRP (B.), Avgust 1917 g-Fevral' 1918 g*. Moscow, 1929.
Joukoff Eudin, Xenia and Fisher, H.H. in collaboration with Brown Jones, R., eds. *Soviet Russia and the West, 1920–1927: A Documentary Survey*. Stanford: Stanford University Press, 1967.
Joukoff Eudin, Xenia and North, Robert C., eds. *Soviet Russia and the East, 1920–1927: A Documentary Survey*. Stanford: Stanford University Press, 1964.
Meijer, Jan M., ed. *The Trotsky Papers, 1917–1922*. London, The Hague, Paris: Mouton & Co., 1964.
Ministerium für Auswärtige Angelegenheiten der DDR-Ministerium für Auswärtige Angelegenheiten der UdSSR. *Deutsch-Sowietische Beziehungen von der Verhandlungen in Brest-Litowsk bis zum Abschluss des Rapallovertrages*. Berlin, 1968.

Ministertsvo Innostrannykh Del SSSR. *Dokumenty Vneshnei Politiki SSSR*. Moscow, 1959.
Scarpa, Gino, ed. *Le Proposte di Pace del Governo Russo: Documenti Diplomatici*. Roma: Istituto Coloniale Italiano, 1920.
The Parliamentary Debates: Official Report, Fifth Series. London, 1919–20.
United States of America, Department of State. *Papers Relating to the Foreign Relations of the United States*. Washington, D.C., 1931.
Woodward, E.L. and Butler, R., eds. *Documents on British Foreign Policy, 1919–1939*, First Series. London, 1947.
Zeman, Z.A.B., ed. *Germany and the Revolution in Russia, 1915–1918: Documents from the Archives of the German Foreign Ministry*. London: Oxford University Press, 1958.

Books

Ascher, Abraham. *The Mensheviks in the Russian Revolution*. Ithscs, N.Y.: Cornell University Press, 1976.
Balabanoff, Angelica. *La mia Vita di Rivoluzionaria*. Milan: Feltrinelli, 1979.
Balabanoff, Angelica. *Lenin visto da vicino*. Rome: Opere Nuove, 1959.
Balabanoff, Angelica. *Ricordi di una Socialista*. Rome: Donatello De Luigi, 1946.
Baumgart, Winfried. *Deutsche Ostpolitik, 1918: Von Brest-Litowsk bis zum Ende des Ersten Weltkrieges*. Vienna and Munich: Oldenbourg, 1966.
Boffa, Giuseppe. *Storia dell'Unione Sovietica*. Milan: Mondadori, 1976.
Bosio, Gianni. *La Grande Paura, Settembre 1920: L'Occupazione delle Fabbriche*. Rome: Samonà e Savelli, 1970.
Bracher, Karl. D. *Zeit der Ideologien*. Stuttgart: Deutsche Verlags-Anstalt, 1982.
Broué, Pierre. *Révolution en Allemagne, 1917–1923*. Paris: Editions de Minuit, 1971.
Callwell, C.E. *Field-Marshal Sir Henry Wilson: His Life and Diaries*. New York: Cassell, 1927.
Carr, Edward. H. *The Bolshevik Revolution, 1917–1923*. London: Macmillan, 1950.
Carr, Edward H. *German-Soviet Relations between the Two World Wars, 1919–1939*. Baltimore: Johns Hopkins Press, 1951.
Carroll, Eber M. *Soviet Communism and Western Opinion, 1919–1921*. Edited by F.B.M. Holliday. Chapel Hill: University of North Carolina Press, 1965.
Chamberlin, William H. *The Russian Revolution, 1917–1921*. New York: Macmillan, 1935.
Coates, William P. and Zelda K. *A History of Anglo-Soviet Relations*, with a preface by D. Lloyd George. London: Lawrence and Wishart, 1943.
Commission of the Central Committee of the C.P.S.U. (B.), ed. *History of the Communist Party of the Soviet Union (Bolshevik): Short Course*. New York: International Publishers, 1939.
Debo, Richard K. *Revolution and Survival: The Foreign Policy of Soviet Russia, 1917–1918*. Toronto: University of Toronto Press, 1979.
Dennis, Alfred L.P. *The Foreign Policies of Soviet Russia*. New York: Dutton and Company, 1924.
Deutscher, Isaac. *Stalin: A Political Biography*. London: Oxford University Press, 1965.
Deutscher, Isaac. *The Prophet Armed: Trotsky, 1879–1921*. London: Oxford University Press, 1954.

Select Bibliography

Dockrill, Michael L. and Douglas Doold, J. *Peace without Promise: Britain and the Peace Conference, 1919–1923*. London: Batsford Academic and Educational, 1981.
Don Levine, Isaac. *Eyewitness to History: Memoirs and Reflections of a Foreign Correspondent for Half a Century*. New York: Hawthorn Books, 1973.
Etherton, Percy T. *In the Heart of Asia*. Boston and New York: Houghton Mifflin, 1926.
Fainsod, Merle. *International Socialism and the World War*. New York: Octagon Books, 1966.
Farnsworth, Beatrice. *William Bullitt and the Soviet Union*. Bloomington, Indiana University Press, 1967.
Filene, Peter G. *Americans and the Soviet Experiment, 1917–1933*. Cambridge, Mass., Harvard University Press, 1967.
Fischer, Louis. *Men and Politics: An Autobiography*. New York: Duell, Sloan and Pearce, 1941.
Fischer, Louis. *The Life of Lenin*. New York: Harper & Row, 1964.
Fischer, Louis. *The Soviets in World Affairs: A History of the Relations between the Soviet Union and the Rest of the World, 1917–1929*. Princeton, N.J.: Princeton University Press, 1951.
Fischer, Ruth. *Stalin and German Communism*. Cambridge, Mass.: Harvard University Press, 1948.
Fraser-Tytler, Sir William K., *Afghanistan: A Study of Political Developments in Central Asia*. London and New York: Oxford University Press, 1950.
Freund, Gerald. *Unholy Alliance: Russian-German Relations from the Treaty of Brest-Litovsk to the Treaty of Berlin*. New York: Harcourt, Brace & Company, 1957.
Frossard, Louis Oscar. *De Jaurès à Leon Blum: Souvenirs d'un Militant*. Paris, Flammarion, 1930.
Geller, Mihail and Nekric, Aleksandr. *Storia dell'URSS dal 1917 a Oggi: L'Utopia al Potere*. Milano: Rizzoli, 1984.
Gibson, Ralf. *Soviet Foreign Policy, 1917–1974*. Sydney: Wentworth Books, 1975.
Gilbert, Martin. *Winston S. Churchill*. London: Heinemann, 1975.
Gorokhov, I., Zamiatin, L. and Zemskov, I. *G.V. Chicherin: Diplomat Leninskoi Skholy*. Moscow, 1966.
Graubard, Stephen R. *British Labour and the Russian Revolution, 1917–1924*. Cambridge, Mass., Harvard University Press, 1956.
Guilbeaux, Henri. *Du Kremlin au Cherche-Midi*. Paris: Gallimard, 1933.
Hard, William. *Raymond Robins' Own Story*. New York and London: Harpers and Brothers, 1920.
Helfferich, Karl T. *Der Weltkrieg*. Karlsruhe, 1925.
Hilger, Gustav and Meyer, Alfred G. *The Incompatible Allies: A Memorial History of German-Soviet Relations, 1918–1941*. New York: Macmillan, 1953.
Hoffmann, Max. *War Diaries and other Papers*. London: Martin Secker, 1929.
Kaplan, Justin. *Lincoln Steffens: A Biography*. New York: Simon & Schuster, 1974.
Kochan, Lionel. *Russia and the Weimar Republic*. Cambridge: Bowes & Bowes, 1954.
König, Helmut. *Lenin un der Italienische Sozialismus, 1915–1921*. Tübingen: Böhlau, 1967.
Korbel, Josef. *Poland between East and West: Soviet and German Diplomacy toward Poland, 1919–1933*. Princeton, N.J.: Princeton University Press, 1963.
Lazitch, Branko and Drachkovitch, Milorad M. *Lenin and the Comintern*. Stanford: Hoover Institution Press, 1972.

Lederer, Ivo J., ed. *Russian Foreign Policy: Essays in Historical Perspective*. New Haven and London: Yale University Press, 1962.
Leggett, George. *The Cheka: Lenin's Political Police*. Oxford: Clarendon Press, 1981.
Lenin, Vladimir I. *Collected Works*. 45 vols. London: Lawrence & Wishart, 1960.
Libbey, James K. *Alexander Gumberg and Soviet-American Relations, 1917–1933*. Lexington: University Press of Kentucky, 1977.
Lockhart, Sir Robert Hamilton Bruce. *The Diaries of Sir Robert Bruce Lockhart, 1915–1938*. Edited by Kenneth Young. London: Macmillan, 1973.
Luxemburg, Rosa. *Scritti Politici*. Edited by Lelio Basso. Rome: Editori Riuniti, 1967.
Mayer, Arno J. *Political Origins of the New Diplomacy, 1917–1918*. New Haven: Yale University Press, 1959.
Melograni, Piero. *Fascismo, Comunismo e Rivoluzione Industriale*. Rome-Bari: Laterza, 1984.
Melograni, Piero. *Storia Politica della Grande Guerra, 1915–1918*. Bari: Laterza, 1969.
Melville, Cecil F. *The Russian Face of Germany: An Account of the Secret Military Relations between the German and Soviet-Russian Governments*. London: Wishart & Co., 1932.
Mitchell, Allan. *Revolution in Bavaria, 1918–1919: The Eisner Regime and the Soviet Republic*. Princeton: Princeton University Press, N.J., 1965.
Nicolson, Harold. *Curzon: The Last Phase, 1919–1925: A Study in Post-War Diplomacy*. New York: Harcourt, Brace and Co., 1974.
Page, Stanley W. *Lenin and World Revolution*. New York: New York University Press, 1959.
Petracchi, Giorgio. *La Russia Rivoluzionaria nella Politica Italiana: Le Relazioni Italo-Sovietiche, 1917–1925*. Rome-Bari: Laterza, 1982.
Philips Price, Morgan. *My Reminiscences of the Russian Revolution*. London: George Allen and Unwin, 1921.
Pipes, Richard. *The Formation of the Soviet Union: Communism and Nationalism, 1917–1923*. Cambridge, Mass., 1964.
Rabenau, Friedrich von. *Seeckt: Aus seinem Leben, 1918–1936*. Leipzig: Hase & Koehler, 1940.
Radek, Karl B. *Zur Taktik des Kommunismus: Ein Schreiben an den Oktober-Parteitag der KPD*. Hamburg, 1919.
Riddell, George A. *Lord Riddell's Intimate Diary of the Peace Conference and after, 1918–1923*. London: Gollancz, 1933.
Riekhoff, Harald von. *German-Polish Relations, 1918–1933*. Baltimore and London: Johns Hopkins Press, 1971.
Robien, Louis de. *Journal d'un Diplomate en Russie, 1917–1918*. Paris: Albin Michel, 1967.
Romanelli, Guido. *Nell'Ungheria di Bela Kun e durante l'Occupazione Militare Romena: La mia Missione, Maggio-Novembre 1919*. Udine: Doretti, 1964.
Rowland, Peter. *Lloyd George*. London: Barrie and Jenkins, 1975.
Russell, Bertrand. *The Practice and Theory of Bolshevism*. London: Allen and Unwin, 1920.
Salvemini, Gaetano. "Lezioni di Harvard: L'Italia dal 1919 al 1929", in *Scritti sul Fascismo*. vol. 1. Edited by Roberto Vivarelli. Milan: Feltrinelli, 1961.
Scheidemann, Philipp. *The Making of New Germany: The Memoirs of Philipp Scheidemann*. New York: Appleton & Co., 1929.
Serra, Enrico. *Nitti e la Russia*. Bari: Dedalo, 1975.

Solzhenitsyn, Aleksandr. *Lenin in Zurich*. New York: Farrar, Straus and Giroux, 1976.
Spector, Ivar. *The First Russian Revolution: Its Impact on Asia*. Englewood Cliffs, N.J.: Prentice-Hall, 1962.
Spriano, Paolo. *Storia del Partito Comunista Italiano: Da Bordiga a Gramsci*. Turin: Einaudi, 1967.
Stalin, Joseph V. *Works*. Moscow: Foreign Languages Publishing House, 1953.
Steed, Henry W. *Through Thirty Years*. London: Heinemann, 1924.
Suchanov, Nikolaj N. *Zapiski O Revoljutsii*. Berlin, St. Petersburg and Moscow, 1923.
Trotsky, Lev D. *My Life: An Attempt at an Autobiography*. New York: Scribner's Sons, 1930.
Trotsky, Lev D. *The History of the Russian Revolution*. Ann Arbor: University of Michigan Press, 1961.
Trotsky, Lev D. *Stalin: An Appraisal of the Man and his Influence*. New York and London: Harper & Brothers, 1941.
Tumulty, Joseph P. *Woodrow Wilson as I Know Him*. Garden City, N.J., and Toronto: Doubleday, Page & Co., 1921.
Ulam, Adam B. *Expansion and Coexistence: The History of Soviet Foreign Policy, 1917–1973*. New York: Praeger, 1974.
Ulam, Adam B. *The Bolsheviks: The Intellectual and Political History of the Triumph of Communism in Russia*. New York: Macmillan, 1965.
Ullman, Richard H. *Anglo-Soviet Relations, 1917–1921*, vol. 3, *The Anglo-Soviet Accord*. Princeton, N.J., 1972.
Varga, Eugen, *La Dictature du Proletariat: Problèmes Economiques*. Paris: L'Humanité, 1922.
Wohl, Robert. *French Communism in the Making, 1914–1924*. Stanford: Stanford University Press, 1966.
Zeman, Z.A.B. and Scharlau, W.B. *The Merchant of Revolution: The Life of Alexander Israel Helphand (Parvus), 1867–1924*. London: Oxford University Press, 1965.
Zetkin, Clara. *Reminiscences of Lenin*. New York: International Publishers, 1934.

Articles

Ascher, Abraham. "Russian Marxism and the German Revolution, 1917–1920." *Archiv für Sozialgeschichte*, 6–7 (1967): 391–439.
Bradley, J.F.N. "France, Lenin and the Bolsheviks." *English Historical Review*, 86 (1971): 783–789.
Carr, Edward H. "Radek's 'Political Salon' in Berlin, 1919." *Soviet Studies*, 3 (1952): 411–430.
Debo, Richard K. "Litvinov and Kamenev, Ambassadors Extraordinary: The Problems of Soviet Representation Abroad." *Slavic Review*, (September, 1975): 463–482.
Himmer, Robert. "Soviet Policy toward Germany during the Russo-Polish War, 1920." *Slavic Review*, (December, 1976): 665–682.
Kobliakov, I.K. "Bor'ba Sovetskogo Gosudartsva za Sokhranenie Mira s Germaniei v Period Deistviia Brestkogo Dogovora, Mai-Noiabr' 1918." *Istoria SSSR*, 4 (1958): 3–26.

Lerner, Warren. "Poland in 1920: A Case Study in Foreign-Policy Decision Making under Lenin." *South Atlantic Quarterly*, 72, n. 3 (Summer 1973): 406–414.
Monteleone, Renato. "Il Partito Comunista Austriaco: Rapporti e Corrispondenza con gli Italiani nel Primo Dopoguerra." *Movimento Operaio e Socialista*, (July–September, 1972): 5–115.
Radek, Karl B. "Deutschland und Russland." *Die Zukunft*, 7 February 1920, 178–189.
Radek, Karl B. "November." *Krasnaya Nov'*, (October, 1926): 139–175.
Silone, Ignazio. "Come Ricordo Lenin." *Corriere della Sera*, 22 April 1970, p. 3.
Smith, Arthur L. "The German General Staff and Russia, 1919–1926." *Soviet Studies*, (October, 1956): 125–133.
Valiani, Leo. "La Politica Estera dei Governi Rivoluzionari Ungheresi del 1918–1919." *Rivista Storica Italiana* (December, 1966): 888–911.

Index

Afghanistan, 80, 107
Agosti, Aldo, 58
Alekseev, Mikhail Vasilievich, 25
Alessandri, Cesare, 72
Amanullah, Emir, 80
Andreyev, Nikolay, 23
Armand, Inessa, 11
Asia, 84
   Soviet policy in, 77–81, 87–90
   Soviet propaganda in, 105, 107–10

Balabanova, Angelica, 56, 58, 71–72, 76, 78
Balfour, Arthur J., 105
Bauer, Max, 68
Berlin, Treaties of (1918), 21–26
Bettelheim, Ernoe, 61
Black Hundreds, 101–2
Bliumkin, Iakov, 23
Bolshevik party
   Brest-Litovsk Treaty and, 6
   German aid to, 9–14
   German rapprochement with, 17–19
   Luxemburg on, 31, 33–34
   at time of Russian Revolution, 1–3
   in World War I, 4
   see also Communist party (Soviet Union)
Bombacci, Nicola, 95
Bordiga, Amadeo, 122
Brest-Litovsk, Treaty of (1917), 4–7, 15, 31
Bronski, M.G., 19, 120–21
Broué, Pierre, 29–30, 35
Bryant, Louise, 50
Buckler, William H., 46
Bukharin, Nikolai I., 5–6, 22, 70
Bullitt, William, 50–53, 59, 83, 85

Cabrini, Angiolo, 95

Cachin, Marcel, 121, 122
Campa, Odorado, 95
Carr, Edward H., 64
Carroll, E.M., 84
Chamberlin, W.H., 21
Chicherin, Georgy V.
   Asian policy of, 78
   Berlin Treaties and, 19, 24, 25
   on British policy on Soviets, 86
   Bullitt and, 51–53
   Comintern founding and, 55, 57
   concessions offered by, 44–46, 50
   on end of economic blockade, 93
   as Foreign Commissar, 15–16
   foreign policy of, 122
   German Social Democrats and, 28–29
   Hungarian revolution and, 62
   Italian recognition and, 74
   on Krasin-Lloyd George talks, 104, 106–9
   Russo-Polish War and, 112–14, 118
Churchill, Winston, 47, 63–64, 84, 85, 87, 114
Clemenceau, Georges, 46, 85, 91
Comintern, 55–58, 70, 71
   Second Congress of, 78–79, 121–22
Communist party (Italy), 122
Communist party (Poland), 97–98
Communist party (Soviet Union), 55, 57, 12
   see also Bolshevik party
Constitutional-Democratic party (Cadets; Russia), 40
Curzon, George Nathaniel, 86, 91, 104–5, 112–13, 115
Curzon Line, 103
Czernin (count, Austro-Hungarian Empire), 17

Danishevsky, 118
Degot, W., 72, 73
Denikin, Anton Ivanovich, 85, 91
Deutscher, Isaac, 9
Dzerzhinsky, Feliks Edmundovich, 5

Eberlein, Hugo, 34, 55, 56
Ebert, Friedrich, 3, 27
Estonia, 93–94
executions, 40
Eyre, Lincoln, 92–93

Fischer, Louis, 16, 25, 44, 93
Fischer, Ruth, 68
Foch, Ferdinand, 85, 111
France
  Krasin-Lloyd George talks and, 107
  Russo-Polish peace talks and, 114–17
  Russo-Polish War and, 111
  trade between Soviet Union and, 95
Fuerstenberg, Jacob (Hanecki), 10–13, 22

Gayda, Virginio, 95
Germany
  Berlin Treaties and, 21–26
  Brest-Litovsk Treaty and, 5, 6
  defeat in World War I of, 27–28
  Kopp's talks in, 113
  Lenin and Bolsheviks aided by, 9–14
  Lenin's policy toward, 16
  post-World War I, 28–29
  Radek as Soviet "representative" in, 67–70
  rapprochements between Russia and, 16–19, 63–66
  revolution in, 29–35
  Russo-Polish War and, 99–101, 103
  Soviet post-World War I policy toward, 43
  at time of Russian Revolution, 2, 3
Gorchakov (prince, Russia), 78
Grabsky, Wladyslaw, 111
Gramsci, Antonio, 1, 50
Gravina, Manfredi, 75–76

Great Britain
  Asia and, 77
  Krasin's talks in, 104–10
  negotiations between Soviet Union and, 91
  peace with Soviet Union sought by, 45–47, 83–84
  Russo-Polish War and, 103–4, 111–18
  Soviet Union invaded by, from Persia, 79

Haase, Hugo, 28–29
Hanecki (Jacob Fuerstenberg), 10–13, 22
Harden, Maximilian, 68
Helfferich, Karl, 23, 24
Helphand, Alexander Israel (Parvus), 9–13
Hilger, Gustav, 66, 100
House, Edward Mandell, 52, 64
Hungary, revolution in (1918–19), 59–62
Hunt, Frazier, 49–50

Independent Social Democratic party (Germany), 28–30
India, 88
Ioffe, Adolf Abramovich, 17, 18, 21–22, 28, 44
Italy, 105
  Communist party formed in, 122
  revolutionaries in, 72–76
  Russo-Polish War and, 103
  trade between Soviet Union and, 95–96

Kamenev, Lev, 43, 115–18, 119
Kaplan, Fanja, 26, 40
Kautsky, Karl, 30
Kobilinsky, Michail, 95
Kolchak, Aleksandr Vasilievich, 84, 91, 94
Kopp, Viktor, 65–66, 70, 100–101, 113
Kozlowski, 12
Krasin, Leonid, 22, 95
  British trade talks with, 119

Lloyd George and, 104–10, 111
Russo-Polish peace talks and,
115–17
Kun, Bela, 59–62, 78

Lansing, Robert, 50
Larin, 22
Left Socialist Revolutionary party
(Russia), 23, 40
Lenin, V.I.
Asian policies of, 78–80
attempted assassination of, 26
Berlin Treaties and, 21, 25
Brest-Litovsk Treaty and, 4–7
on Bukharin, 70
Bullitt and, 51–53
Comintern founding and, 55–58
cult of, 123
on end of economic blockade,
92–93
on Estonia peace treaty, 93–94
foreign policies of, 43–47, 89, 122
German aid to, 9–13, 16, 18–19
Hungarian revolution and, 60–62
Italian revolutionaries and, 72–76
on Krasin-Lloyd George talks, 106
letter to London *Times* from, 109
Luxemburg and, 30–35
Mirbach's murder and, 23
post-World War I Germany and,
27–30
on Prinkipo meeting, 50
during Russian Revolution, 1–3
on Russo-Polish peace talks, 118
Russo-Polish War and, 97–99,
101–2, 112, 113
at Second Comintern Congress, 121
Soviet state organized by, 37–41
on trade relations, 96, 120
Trotsky and, 15
Levi, Paul, 70
Levine, Isaac Don, 52–53
Liebknecht, Karl, 29–30, 33–35
Lithuania, 112
Litvinov, Maksim
Bullitt's meeting with, 51, 52
Comintern founding and, 57
concessions offered by, 45, 46

on global revolution, 27
Lloyd George and, 91, 95
in peace negotiations, 86, 87
on revolution in Italy, 75–76
Lloyd George, David
Bullitt's mission and, 50, 52, 59
on end of economic blockade,
94–95
Krasin and, 104–10
negotiations between Litvinov and,
91
peace with Soviet Union sought by,
45, 46, 83–87
Russo-Polish peace talks and,
114–18, 119
Russo-Polish War and, 103–4,
111–14
on Soviet-German alliance, 64
Ludendorff, Erich Friedrich Wilhelm,
17, 24
Luxemburg, Rosa, 28, 30–35, 56

Malone, Cecil B., 53, 85
Markhlevsky, Julian, 98
Martov, Iulii, 31
Marx, Karl, 1
Menshevik movement, 31–32
Meyer, Ludwig, 45
Millerand, Alexandre, 94, 95, 107,
111, 114–16
Moor, Karl, 68
Müller, Hermann, 65, 100

Nadeau, Ludovic, 52
Nansen, F., 52
newspapers, 38
Nitti, Francesco Saverio, 73–75, 91,
94–96

O'Grady, James, 86, 87
Orlando, Vittorio Emanuele, 46, 64

Paderewski, Ignacy Jan, 84
Paquet, Alphonse, 69
Paris Peace Conference (1918), 49
Parvus (Alexander Israel Helphand),
9–13
Pasha, Enver, 65, 67

Pasha, Kemal, 80
Pasha, Talaat, 67
Patek, Stanislaw, 111
Perri, Francesco, 75
Persia (Iran), 79–80, 89, 107
Petlyura, Simon, 97
Pilsudski, József, 97, 108
Plekhanov, Georgi Valentinovich, 11
Poland, 64, 84
  in Russo-Polish War, 97–102, 103–5, 107, 111–18, 119
Preziosi, Gabriele, 105
Price, Morgan Philips, 25, 28
Prinkipo meeting (proposed; 1918), 49–50, 83

Radek, Karl, 11, 12
  on Berlin Treaties, 25
  at Comintern founding, 56
  German revolution and, 27–28, 32–34
  in Germany, 67–70
  Italian revolutionaries and, 72
  on Soviet foreign policy, 88–90
Rakovsky, Cristian, 51, 62
Rathenau, Walter, 68
Reed, John, 119
Reza Khan, 80
Riddell, Lord George Allardice, 104, 114, 115
Robien, Louis de, 4
Roy, M.N., 79, 122
Russia. *See also* Soviet Union
  Brest-Litovsk Treaty and, 4–7
  German rapprochement with, 16–19
  organization of Soviet state in, 37–41
  in World War I, 3–4
Russian Revolution, 1
Russo-Polish War, 97–102, 103–5, 107, 111–18, 119

Salvemini, Gaetano, 72
San Remo Conference (1920), 104, 105
Scharlau, W.B., 9
Scheidermann, Philipp, 3

Schliapnikov, 2–3
Second International, 57
Serrati, Giacinto Menotti, 71, 72, 74–75, 122
Silone, Ignazio, 61
Sklyansky, 112
Skrypnik, 2
Smuts, Jan, 59–60
Social Democratic party (Germany), 28–29
Socialist party (Italy), 123
Sokolnikov, Grigori Yakovievich, 22
Sokolovska, Elena, 72, 73
Soviet Union. *See also* Russia
  Asia and, 77–81
  civil war in, 53
  economic blockade ended against, 91–96
  Great Britain and, 83–90
  Hungarian revolution and, 59
  Lenin's organization of, 37–41
  post-World War I foreign policy, 43–47
  rapprochement between Germany and, 63–66
  recognized by Italy, 73–74
  in Russo-Polish War, 97–102, 103–4, 107, 111–18, 119
Spa (Belgium) Conference (1920), 111
Spartacus League (Germany), 31, 33, 34
Stalin, Joseph, 6, 40, 77, 112, 118
Steed, Henry Wickham, 52
Steinhardt, Karl, 55, 56
Steklov, Iury, 29
Sufi, Mustafa, 80
Sultan-Galiev, M., 80
Sverdlov, 2

Third International (Comintern), 55–58. *See also* Comintern
Toman, Karl, 74–75
Trotsky, Leon, 50, 93
  on Asian agitation, 78, 106
  on Bolshevik revolution, 3
  Brest-Litovsk Treaty and, 4, 6
  disputes between Lenin and, 5
  German-Soviet peace and, 17

Luxemburg on, 33
Parvus and, 9
on peaceful coexistence, 119
resigned as Foreign Commissar, 15
on Russo-Polish War, 98, 112, 113
Turati, Filippo, 75, 121, 122
Turkey, 80–81, 90

United States, 46–47, 50–53
Uritsky, Moisey, 5

Varga, Eugene, 60
Vatsetis, Joakim I., 61–62
Versailles, Treaty of (1919), 63, 83
   Poland under, 98–100
   Russo-Polish War and, 118
Virgili, Giovanni Amadori, 95
von Baden, Max, 28
von Bergen, Diego, 13–14
von Hintze, Paul, 23, 24, 68
von Kühlmann, Richard, 13, 16–19, 22
von Maltzan, Ago, 100
von Mirbach-Harff, Wilhelm, 17–19, 23
von Reibnitz, Eugen Freiherr, 68

von Seeckt, Hans, 64–66, 68, 99–100
von Simons, Walter, 101
Vorovsky, V.C., 45, 55

Wilhelm II (kaiser, Germany), 11, 16, 17, 23, 27
Wilson, Sir Henry, 117
Wilson, Woodrow, 44–47, 49–52, 84
World War I, 3–4, 15
   Berlin Treaties and, 21–26
   Brest-Litovsk Treaty and, 4–7
   end of, 27
   German aid to Bolsheviks during, 9–14
   German-Russian rapprochement during, 16–19
   Treaty of Versailles to end, 63
Wrangel, Pëtr Nikolaevich, 108, 110, 112, 118

Yudenich, Nikolai Nikolaevich, 85, 91

Zeman, Z.A.B., 9
Zetkin, Clara, 70
Zinoviev, Grigori Evseevich, 56, 76, 78